COUNTDOWN

WILL YOU RUN OUT OF MONEY BEFORE YOU RUN OUT OF TIME?

RANDALL N. SMITH
GREGORY L. REED

A Division of PUBLISH for Success

This publication is designed to provide general information regarding the subject matter covered. Because each individual's legal, tax and financial situation is different, specific advice should be tailored to the particular circumstances. For this reason, the reader is advised to consult with his or her own attorney, accountant and/or other advisor regarding the individual's specific situation. The authors have taken reasonable precautions in the preparation of this book and believe that the information presented in the book is accurate as of the date it was written. However, neither the authors or publisher assumes any responsibility for any errors or omissions. The authors and publisher specifically disclaim any liability resulting from the use or application of the information contained in this book, and the information is not intended to serve as legal, tax or other financial advice related to individual situations. Case in Point discussions are for informational purposes only and may not be representative of the experiences of other clients. Illustrations are hypothetical and are not intended to represent or project actual performance or results.

PFS Books
Division of PUBLISH for Success
2000 E. Arapaho Road, Suite 4104
Richardson, Texas 75081
Visit our website at www.publishforsuccess.com

ISBN   0-9769355-0-3

FIRST EDITION: November 2005

COUNTDOWN

Dr. Lee,

    Thank you for your consideration of our firm for your planning needs. We trust you will find our book a good use of your time. It's an easy read on purpose, since you are *time-starved* as it is.

             Enjoy

1-20-2006

CONTENTS

ACKNOWLEDGEMENTS

As is probably the case with every book that has ever been written, there are many people deserving of credit whose help was essential to completing this project. There are three distinct groups, who played crucial roles, and who, at the very least, deserve acknowledgment.

First, we owe a debt of gratitude to the hundreds of clients who put their trust in us and offered feedback that ultimately helped us formulate what would become Prosprus™.

Second, there are many people who played major roles in shaping our careers and helping us become the best we can be. Without the assistance of these professionals, this project would never have even been considered.

Finally, there are those who significantly helped by shaping and adding professional assistance in refining the final outcome.

A few of those deserving of credit are Ted Frank, Chris Fay, Frank Voigt, Jet Parker, Pam Carvey, Jeff Moss and Debby Reed.

To all of these people, we offer a heartfelt "THANK YOU!"

FOREWORD

As the President and CEO of a leading financial services distribution company, I am often called upon to discuss my vision of where the financial services world is headed. Having been in the business for over 20 years, I have witnessed many changes. Financial services have been delivered by professionals who have referred to themselves in many ways – "agents," "brokers," "advisors." Today, it seems that the term of choice is "financial planner." The problem is that the term "financial planner" has been so overused and abused that it barely has any meaning anymore.

Financial planning is a lot more than selling investments or insurance products. It is also more than just a record of what a client has done in the past and should do in the future.

Real financial planning is all that and much, much more.

Traditionally, financial planners who actually performed true financial planning created a nice financial plan and bound it in a nice leather portfolio. Good information was provided, but the client's life was not changed because the implementation of the plan was left to the client. The client did not really identify with the plan on an emotional level. He or she understood on an intellectual level, but rarely does someone take specific action based solely on knowledge.

In *Countdown*, Randy Smith and Greg Reed have mapped out their vision of how financial planning should be conducted. Through their financial planning process, called Prosprus™, they have moved the process from a decades-old static model to an interactive and dynamic one that engages both sides of the brain: intellectual and emotional.

Countdown describes a system that is designed to offer clients the ability to see virtually any scenario they can think of and the impact on their financial plans. No longer are clients confined to one set of static assumptions. What happens if returns are lower than history has shown? What if health expenses continue to inflate at a rate much higher than the rate of inflation? What if the client retires at 60 vs. 65? Now clients don't have to wonder.

With 76 million Baby Boomers nearing retirement, the timing of this book could not be better. I hope that you will not only read this book, but also take action to ensure that your financial house is in order. If you are serious about changing your life, this book is a great road map to begin your journey.

Jessica Bibliowicz
President and CEO
National Financial Partners

INTRODUCTION

You will work for decades toward one goal: retirement. And in your mind, you likely have a vision of your desired lifestyle during those hard-earned retirement years.

Yet people just like you are shocked to learn that retirement simply will not meet their expectations. Why? No matter what their current earnings, even wealthy individuals likely have not created a financial future that will fulfill their dreams.

The reason is simple. Most financial-planning methods fail. Unfortunately, victims don't discover their plans' shortcomings until it is too late. They run out of money before they run out of time. The result is an unsatisfying lifestyle during retirement, or worse, financial crisis.

We all face the same mortal countdown. Can you ensure your financial security, as well as the lifestyle you crave? Today, you have the power to choose. The book you hold can be priceless. Why? Because it will change the way you look at financial planning. Plus, it will arm you with the tools to meet your lifestyle goals.

Forget conventional financial-planning methods, which typically apply the same formulaic, fill-in-the-blanks process to everyone. These generic financial plans rely on a process that is exactly backward. The client is expected to gather up reams of extensive financial data and deliver it to his or her financial planner. The planner then creates a plan without engaging the client in the process. The resulting plan lacks customization. It is packaged in a stagnant three-ring binder. And it does not provide triggers to change behavior and execute the plan. The client receives this document, yet typically doesn't know what to do next. The financial planner might recommend the purchase of life insurance, mutual funds or other investments from specific companies, allegedly to help accomplish the goals of the plan. But in the end, the client is left with little more than a stack of useless paper and no progress. Sound familiar?

Think of most financial planning like a diet. A busy executive maintains bad financial habits for years. Suddenly, when a loved one dies or a potential crisis looms, he gains a sense of mortality. Financial planning takes on new importance. But rather than changing his financial lifestyle, the client goes through a difficult financial-planning "diet." He rushes to make some kind of positive change. But before too long, he slips back into his old "I'll think about it later" habits – just like the dieter returning to corn chips and soda.

Good financial planning doesn't carry the difficulty or pain of a diet. It's a true lifestyle change – painless, automatic and positive. There are a lot of things that financial planners could do to make their clients' lives easier and to make financial planning less of a chore, but most don't do it. They leave all the "heavy lifting" up to their clients and then shake their heads in wonderment when the client doesn't follow through on the plan. This is exactly backward. Like most other service providers, the financial planner should be the one doing the heavy lifting and execution, and letting the client do what he or she does best – make decisions.

Typical Financial Plan	Advanced Financial Plan
After the static, paper-based plan is created, the client remembers a key element that was not included – an inheritance, an asset or an upcoming expense. Yet the plan cannot be modified without the investment of more time and money.	The plan leverages financial software that can be easily updated and changed. Any time a significant life event occurs, the plan can immediately reflect its impact and the results can be viewed by the client real-time from any computer.
The plan produces a large to-do list for the client, who typically doesn't have the time, expertise or motivation to work through each and every step.	The plan makes recommendations to the client, who is then assisted by professionals who can implement it.
The financial planner recommends specific products, from life insurance to annuities and investments. The client questions the value of the specific recommendations, because the planner likely receives commissions for selling certain products.	The financial planner shows the client several ways to reach his or her ultimate goals. The client chooses his or her preferred path, including the types of financial products he or she would like to purchase, if any. The client drives the process rather than the other way around. This builds trust between advisor and client.

Consider the stark differences between a typical personal financial plan and one that can change and grow with you. Do any of the scenarios in the chart on the previous page sound familiar? Those scenarios fit most typical clients of personal financial planners.

What if financial planning could spring to life, right before your eyes? What if you could easily see and understand how today's financial decisions affect you in 10, 20 or even 30 years? What if you could change numbers on the fly for different scenarios?

What if you could see it without plowing through stacks of mind-numbing financial spreadsheets?

With this book, you can achieve a new vision of your financial future and ensure that your countdown to and through retirement is fulfilling and not scary. To accomplish this, the book is divided into two sections:

- Part 1 outlines a ground-breaking strategy for financial planning. This section explores the barriers to your success, explains workable solutions and reveals how you can reach your goals. It will provide a financial snap-shot of your future, revealing how much money will be available and whether it will support your desired lifestyle. It will introduce you to a smarter and faster way of making decisions about your future.

- Part 2 delves into the nuts and bolts of personal finance. There you can access detailed explanations of specific strategies, from insurance and investments to trusts and more. It will help you make better decisions for yourself and your family.

Do not let another day pass. Take control of your personal finances now. Get the full picture of how much money you need and how it will create the lifestyle you wish to achieve. And, boost your future net worth potentially by millions. It's easier than you think. Just keep reading.

PART 1

A NEW VIEW OF FINANCIAL PLANNING

If a financial plan is printed and placed in a three-ring binder, is it really worth anything? After all, it cannot change. It cannot be used to show the impact of a purchase or investment decision on your future. It just sits there, reminding you of how far you must travel to meet your goals.

But what if financial planning centered around change? What if it could offer long-term analysis of the specific, real-world financial decisions you make each day?

The answer to these questions is Prosprus™, a financial planning process that enables you to:

- actively participate in the planning process with your financial planner

- clearly understand your financial situation by seeing your net worth depicted in real-time graphics, not in meaningless columns of numbers

- instantly view how your future could be impacted by life events, such as the death of a business partner, a long-term illness, lower investment returns or natural disasters

- create a better future by determining the best products and methods for offsetting disaster, such as insurance, a new savings plan or a reduction in expenditures

With Prosprus you can use your financial present to engineer your financial future. Experience the Prosprus process first-hand by visiting www.prosprus.com before reading this book. Compare your earlier, frustrating, inefficient methods with the future of financial planning.

POWER UP PRODUCTIVITY

---

*"No person will make a great business who wants to do it all himself
or get all the credit."*
ANDREW CARNEGIE

THE DILEMMA

At work, you have a support staff. At home, you don't. So how do you
ensure that your personal affairs operate efficiently?

Case in Point

*Our client has become one of America's most successful inventors. His
ingenious novelty products adorn homes and offices across the nation. Not only is he
a master of great ideas, but he is also an accomplished businessman with a remark-
able track record. Like so many busy executives, he serves effectively as company
visionary, product inventor, industry expert and corporate leader. Our imaginative
client credits his sensational support staff. He delegates to a team that manages the
details, so he can oversee the company's performance.*

*At home, it is another story. This same client finds it hard to manage the
success he has achieved. There just never seems to be enough time to get everything
done. Investments need to be managed. Estate planning documents need to be
created and executed. Life and health insurance need to be reviewed. Without a
team to delegate these critical responsibilities to at home, he doesn't get them done —
for years. This jeopardizes his financial health and compromises the well-being of
his family's future.*

YOUR CONCERN

This successful businessman's situation is very common. Financial planners hear the same story time and again. Most financial planners try to force-fit executives into the current industry system. But there is a better approach: fit the financial planning system around the executive.

Before discussing the details, let's talk about you. The fact that you are reading this book suggests that you are a high-net-worth individual or, due to your commitment to education, hard work and tenacity, you likely will be one in the near future. You are probably a business owner, a highly compensated C-level officer or a high-performing professional on the way up the corporate ladder.

You most likely enjoy what you do for a living; in fact, you are probably passionate about what you do. You are enthusiastic about your company whether you own it, or are a stockholder, a partner or an executive. Time is your most valuable commodity, and you never seem to have enough of it. However, you have learned to leverage time through your ability to delegate.

Delegation enables you to reduce excessive amounts of information into convenient formats. By spending time and effort analyzing only the most critical data, you can accomplish more tasks on a timely basis. All in all, you are pretty efficient in the work environment you have created.

But if you are like most executives, you are likely as inefficient outside the business environment as you are efficient inside it.

Think about it for a minute. At work, you've introduced systems to automatically trigger processes and initiate procedures. Rarely do you have to worry about your next step because you have a team to help you oversee it. You gather information proficiently. You competently finish what you start, and you diligently prioritize. So it begs the question: what happens to you on the drive home? Somehow, all those efficiencies disappear. Crucial details are left incomplete or not even addressed. Deficiencies in the management of your personal financial affairs are so shocking that you would never tolerate similar performance at the office.

THE SOLUTION

Most executives would never allow the inefficiencies that plague their personal financial lives to invade their businesses. Therefore, why do so many business people allow their messy financial situation at home to persist?

After puzzling over the question for years, the answer has become clear. These very successful people learned to leverage time by delegating at work. But when they turned out the lights and stepped outside their businesses, there was no one to whom they could delegate. In fact, their situation was reversed. At home, these high-powered executives were being delegated to by spouses, children and – if they were old enough and lucky enough – grand-children. The reasons were clear. When asked to choose between complet-ing a will or going to a soccer game, they correctly picked the soccer game. That is why Prosprus is designed around executives and their lifestyles.

The Prosprus process enables you to be as productive at home as you are at work by:

- optimizing your time

- streamlining your financial implementation process

- providing you with the support staff to carry out your personal financial planning objectives, just as your work staff helps you carry out your professional financial planning

This approach creates the same efficiency-driven environment outside the office as in the office. You simply delegate action items to a team of specialists. The team implements your strategies, and you reach your goals.

KEY QUESTIONS

1. Are you putting off creating a financial plan because there is no one to help you execute it?

2. Is your personal financial plan as comprehensive as your business plan?

3. Have you spent time preparing for contingencies at home as well as you have prepared for them at work?

4. Have you made yourself and your family the proper priorities, or does work receive *all* your best efforts?

CHAPTER 2

TRUST

"You can never give complete authority and overall power to anyone until trust can be proven."
BILL COSBY

THE DILEMMA

It's hard to trust your financial future to someone you just met.

Case in Point

I love clothes. My wife and friends even kid me because I enjoy shopping for fine clothing so much. A knowledgeable salesperson makes the experience even better. There is nothing more satisfying, however, than a salesperson who cares more about me than the sale and has the integrity to tell me the truth.

For example, I was trying on clothes one day and came out of the dressing room. One of the salespeople looked at me and said, "Randy, it's a nice suit, but it doesn't wear well on you." This was a salesperson who was more concerned about my happiness with the purchase than how he would benefit. This was the beginning of a trust-based relationship.

YOUR CONCERN

A 2002 survey conducted by Forrester, Inc. revealed that "some companies have been more successful than others at earning trust – but even the best have won over only slightly more than half of consumers." Unfortunately, there are far too many financial planners who compromise their integrity. They put little value in building, much less sustaining, trust-based relationships. Yet in the financial planning industry, where people divulge some of their most personal financial information, trust is paramount.

Trust-based behavior should be delivered as part of every business transaction. High-quality financial advisors work to build trust from the very beginning by immediately signing a confidentiality agreement with prospective clients. This is rare in the financial planning world, but it should not be.

Unbeknownst to most consumers, the financial planning industry has several ways to compensate its practitioners. One option is *fee-only advice*. This type of arrangement involves charging fees only for services; advisors are not compensated by commissions on sales. At the other end of the spectrum is *commission-only advice*. Under this system, the advisor is compensated only via the sale of a product. If there is no sale, there is no compensation. Finally, there are planners who receive both *fees and commissions*.

The mixed fee-and-commission approach works best for most people. Why? Because they prefer to tell their stories only one time. During a fee-based, financial planning session, a client can explain where he or she is today, as well as where he or she would like to be in the future. From that information, a customized plan is created to spell out exactly what actions are needed to meet the client's goals. This plan includes a list of recommendations, a small percentage of which will require the purchase of a financial product.

At this point, most clients prefer that their financial advisor assist with these purchases. The client does not want to go to his or her life insurance agent, or worse yet find one, to purchase any insurance the advisor might have discovered was needed. In addition, most financial planning sessions result in new investment recommendations. After a detailed financial analysis, the client usually feels confident in the strategy and wants the financial advisor to take on the challenge. Clients simply do not want to tell their whole story again. They are way too busy for that.

Most clients also prefer calling a single phone number to access all the experts who have created and implemented their financial plans. Therefore, by choosing single-source financial planners who work on both *fee and commission*, clients can be confident that their financial plans and solutions will be implemented in a timely, efficient and accurate manner.

In the end, it all comes down to trust.

THE SOLUTION

Look for independent advisors. Independent advisors have a universe of products to review and utilize on your behalf. Most importantly, their loyalty is to you, not to a particular company or product line. By maintaining independence, financial planners are rewarded for doing what is best for their clients, rather than doing what earns them more money.

To further a trust-based relationship, the planning process should objectively reveal the optimal options that clients should consider at each decision-making juncture. This can be effectively accomplished by Prosprus. This technology-driven planning process provides the client with an *insider's* view of all the financial decisions that many planners tend to conceal.

Prosprus puts you, the client, in the driver's seat, and the financial planner serves as the guide.

The Prosprus process:

- allows you to explore almost every situation that could impact your life, instead of assuming your advisors have done so

- enables you to *spontaneously* review issues that impact your life to ensure that the data, and your options, are not manipulated

- removes biased decision-making, so the plan is not designed around incentives for the planner but rather on how you will benefit most from particular products or investment strategies

- calculates the impact in *future-time* dollars, rather than present-time dollars, by confirming the real value of client money based on projected returns, economic fluctuations and inflation

- diminishes the negative impact of life's hardships by ensuring you choose the right products, rather than presuming a planner has chosen the best ones for you

- eliminates the chance that you will have a canned, fill-in-the-blanks plan used for everyone because Prosprus yields a custom plan to fit your personal needs, goals, life issues, financial limitations and concerns

- eliminates the risk of developing an inferior plan

KEY QUESTIONS

1. Are you using the services of an independent financial planner tied to a specific company and that company's product line?

2. Does your current planning *process* enable you to eliminate information manipulation, whereby you only see what the planner wants you to see rather than the impact of all the options so you can make your own choice?

3. Does the advice you receive feel like the "flavor of the week," rather than advice that is coordinated with your overall financial plan?

4. Do you sometimes leave a meeting with your advisor and wonder why your advisor always offers the products of the same company?

CHAPTER 3

EXCUSE-FREE AND FINANCIALLY FREE

"He that is good for making excuses is seldom good for anything else."
BENJAMIN FRANKLIN

THE DILEMMA

You're diligent about taking care of financial issues at work, but it's difficult to create the same disciplined practices at home.

Case in Point

There was a very successful farmer in the 1920s and 1930s. He built his business the same way most entrepreneurs do: hard work, good decisions and a little good fortune.

Regrettably, luck turned against him during the Great Depression. By the time the economy recovered, he had lost everything. The loss was devastating on both a business and personal level. He never fully recovered.

Until the day he died, the farmer swore that he would never fail like that again. He used what should have been a setback, albeit a very large one, as an excuse to quit. The best way to never lose anything again, he decided, was to avoid owning anything. This "solution" seemed perfectly reasonable to him. For the rest of his life, it was his excuse to never try again.

Think about the legacy he could have left behind had he done things differently. A successful business was built and then destroyed due to economic conditions beyond his control. But he still had time. He could have rebuilt the business. He could have worked very hard and applied the same tenacity that had served him so well the first time around. Likely, his work would have paid off, and the business would have been even more successful the second time around. He could have passed the company on to his children and grandchildren, who could have continued the family business with the same insistence on success. Instead, he allowed a failure to be his excuse, and the generations that followed have been left with nothing more than thoughts of what might have been.

YOUR CONCERN

Making excuses to avoid financial planning can be devastating and lead to future financial hopelessness. Despite this, financial planners hear endless reasons from clients who are avoiding the process. The following are the most common excuses.

"The planning process is too invasive."

It's a common concern: "I'm not telling a complete stranger all about my financial situation." People will reveal their most personal information to buddies on the golf course, divulge embarrassing mishaps to perfect strangers sitting next to them on a plane, and share intimate details about their love lives to their hairstylists. Yet they balk at the idea of communicating financial specifics to a qualified financial planner.

"One plan can't really prepare me for multiple challenges in the future."

Executives often say, "What's the point of creating a financial plan based on four or five life situations, when there are probably dozens I need to worry about in my lifetime?" The majority of financial advisors are still stuck in the three-ring-binder approach to planning. You give them your financial data, and they organize it into a three-ring binder that reflects the four or five standard life situations such as sudden death, disability, birth of a child, college planning, etc. They call that static document a plan.

Enter Prosprus, a technology-driven planning process that enables clients to review and instantly see the effect of 15 to 50 life-changing issues.

"It's too hard to find a good financial planner."

When you are faced with a health crisis, you're not going to let your health deteriorate because it is difficult to find the right specialist. This serious situation requires effort. You would ask your most trusted friends about their experiences with certain doctors. You would request recommendations from your family doctor. You might do some research on the Internet. After narrowing the field to a few experts, you might even interview them.

When it comes to your financial health, should you take the process any less seriously? Ask your senior business associates to recommend trustworthy professionals. Sit down with your accountant or lawyer to find out what financial planning process they've used in the past.

If you're not sure what to look for in a professional financial planner, review the checklist at www.prosprus.com. It's free.

"I'm too busy."

You're too busy to direct the outcome of your financial future? Do you really think so? People make time for what's important to them. Unfortunately, most people don't allocate time for practical wealth management until they have suffered a devastating financial loss or are newly motivated to *make* the time.

Creating the time for financial planning may not be easy, but you'll appreciate the rewards of the effort.

"I had a bad experience with a planner in the past."

Many people have gone through the financial planning process several times, but it didn't work out. They felt taken advantage of by the financial planner.

Many an industry has been marred by the unscrupulous actions of a few. How many times have you heard about a mechanic who took advantage of a customer who knew little about cars? Or a roofer who took advantage of an elderly couple too feeble to confirm claims that the roof was going to cave in if it wasn't "fixed"?

The unprofessional behavior of these people does a disservice to their professions. But by allowing their behavior to dictate your decisions, *you* do a disservice to your future.

Bad things happen. The reason you're successful, and one of the reasons you enjoy success, is that you've learned to isolate failure and move on. Selecting a financial planner, regardless of your previous experiences, should not be the exception to the rule.

THE SOLUTION

Too often, people make excuses to avoid doing something they should. But they could just as easily choose to take action. The Prosprus process makes it easier to make the right choices.

The Prosprus process:

- helps you efficiently create your financial plan, so you are less likely to concoct excuses that you don't have time

- ensures that *you* are involved in designing your own plan, rather than simply being an observer

- motivates you to carry out the steps in your plan

KEY QUESTIONS

1. Are you making excuses for not undertaking a thorough financial planning process?

2. Which do you believe will be more costly to you and your family if a disaster strikes: taking time to make sure your financial matters are handled or continuing to make excuses and hoping that everything will work out?

3. You have never allowed excuses to stand in the way of your professional success, so why should financial planning be any different?

4. Are you allowing a past experience to compromise your family's well-being?

CHAPTER 4

ONE TEAM, ONE PLAN, ONE PERSPECTIVE

"Synergy is the highest activity of life; it creates new untapped alternatives; it values and exploits the mental, emotional, and psychological differences between people."
STEPHEN COVEY

THE DILEMMA

You're diligent about taking care of financial issues at work, but it's difficult to create the same disciplined practices at home.

Case in Point

A career nurse complained about experts not working together in her own industry.

It happens all the time: a family doctor sees a long-time patient and prescribes medication for chronic back pain. The same patient rushes to the emergency room two weeks later because of heart palpitations and receives another prescription, without consideration of what the family doctor has already prescribed. The following month, the patient gets a third prescription from a specialist for arthritis. All this time, the patient's situation is growing worse, rather than better.

The doctors are focusing on the immediate physical problems, rather than the holistic health issues of the patient. As a result, each prescribes a drug that is ideal for that particular ailment, but inappropriate because of interactions with previous prescriptions. Each drug is counteracting the benefits of the others.

In extreme cases, the interactions can be fatal.

YOUR CONCERN

Most people are confounded by the fact that their financial specialists work separately, rather than collectively, to create a single financial vision. This fractionalized approach results in duplication of effort. One process might negate the positive effects of another, perhaps even threatening the long-term viability of the client's financial future.

Does this sound familiar? When you first got out of college, you went beyond needing just a checking account to requiring a savings account as well. A few years later, you purchased your first home and needed a mortgage. This began a business relationship with your banker. Your home purchase necessitated a property and casualty agent. By the time you were 30, you began to get more serious about saving money for the future. Perhaps your banker introduced you to an investment advisor, who recommended that you open an IRA or contribute to a 401(k) plan. Along the way you got married, triggering the need for life insurance and a life insurance agent. In time, you had children and needed an attorney to prepare wills for you and your spouse.

As your career matured, so did your financial situation. Later you sought out someone to prepare your taxes. Your responsibilities got more complicated, and you moved beyond simple tax preparation to hiring a sophisticated tax expert. Eventually your hard work paid off, and you hired a private money manager to take care of your investment portfolio. Finally, you hired a financial planner to complete a comprehensive financial plan. This is all part of the financial lifecycle.

The illustration on the following page demonstrates the natural expansion of service providers as we age.

Here's the clincher: not once in this 40-year span did these financial specialists meet. They all lived and worked in the same region within their own disciplines, cycling in and out of the client's life as needed. And they each impacted the client's financial plan without knowing what the others had recommended. If they were fortunate enough to have met, they often focused on protecting their own best interests, feeling threatened by the other providers instead of using the situation to protect the client's best interests. Sound frightening? It is, and it happens every day.

When people develop a plan, they often do so with little input from their key service providers, such as accountants, investment advisors, insurance agents and the like.

Unfortunately, no one is immune to the lifecycle problem. Consider the example of Jake. Jake's estate planning attorney drew up a new will and couriered it to him for review. The will needed to be signed and notarized before it would be valid. For four years, Jake carried the will in his briefcase as a reminder to have it notarized. His estate planning attorney assumed that

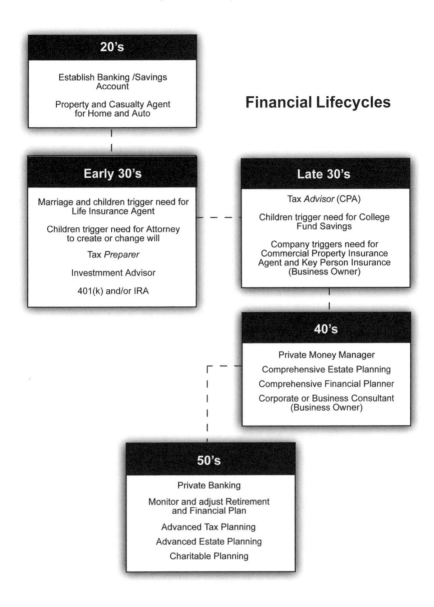

Financial Lifecycles

20's

Establish Banking /Savings Account

Property and Casualty Agent for Home and Auto

Early 30's

Marriage and children trigger need for Life Insurance Agent

Children trigger need for Attorney to create or change will

Tax *Preparer*

Investmment Advisor

401(k) and/or IRA

Late 30's

Tax *Advisor* (CPA)

Children trigger need for College Fund Savings

Company triggers need for Commercial Property Insurance Agent and Key Person Insurance (Business Owner)

40's

Private Money Manager

Comprehensive Estate Planning

Comprehensive Financial Planner

Corporate or Business Consultant (Business Owner)

50's

Private Banking

Monitor and adjust Retirement and Financial Plan

Advanced Tax Planning

Advanced Estate Planning

Charitable Planning

the matter had been handled. But upon reviewing the document, Jake's financial planner discovered that it remained unsigned. Had anything happened to Jake during this time, it could have been financially devastating to his family.

This problem is indicative of the *lifecycle process*, which is triggered when a person must outsource certain responsibilities to specialists. These experts work independently and are often oblivious to the crucial input of the others. These providers are taught to give advice based on the practices within their own disciplines. They look at situations from their own perspectives and they give advice from this narrow view. When advice is isolated from the dynamics of your other experts in this way, it can become dangerous.

THE SOLUTION

In your business, you use a team of specialists who work together to fulfill the vision of your company. Since this approach works at the office, why operate differently at home? The Prosprus process brings all of your personal financial players together to create one master plan that everyone endorses and works to accomplish. Consider this group to be your personal advisory board. Your advisory board acts as a brain trust that can create greater ideas together than each expert can conceive alone. Leveraging an advisory board prevents the isolation of your financial network and increases the odds of realizing your vision.

The Prosprus process:

- results in the development of one coordinated, personal financial plan

- reflects the input of *all* of your advisors

- ensures that the advice of one provider maximizes, rather than compromises, the advice of another

- unites all of your advisors under the direction of your financial planner, who is then held accountable for ensuring the plan is executed

KEY QUESTIONS

1. Is the financial plan you designed based on the collective intelligence of your entire financial advisory team, including your accountant, investment advisor, insurance agent and attorney? Or does it come only from your financial advisor?

2. Are you using a team of specialists that you've outgrown? If so, why?

3. Has your attorney ever met your CPA, specifically to discuss your financial situation?

4. Has your investment advisor changed the account titling of your investment accounts according to the instructions of your attorney?

5. Have the beneficiaries of your life insurance policy been updated per the instructions of your estate planning attorney? Do your other advisors have a copy of your estate plan?

CHAPTER 5

COUNTDOWN

"There cannot be a crisis next week. My schedule is already full."
HENRY KISSINGER

THE DILEMMA

Planning your personal future is as important as planning your professional future, yet you find it nearly impossible to do both.

Case in Point

The absolute necessity of timely financial planning became clear to me many years ago after the tragic death of a client. I had completed a simple needs-analysis for a young couple with two children. The analysis revealed that the couple needed $500,000 in life insurance in the event of the husband's premature death. I ran the numbers to determine the premium for $500,000 of coverage. Unfortunately, the wife decided that the premium was just too much and wanted to purchase $100,000 of coverage instead.

The couple debated whether to buy $500,000 or $100,000 worth of coverage. Ultimately, they decided on the lower premium and chose the $100,000 policy. They understood there could be tragic results if they did not purchase the full amount, but a tragedy was just not going to happen to them. They had a typical "it-won't-happen-to-us" mentality.

A short time later, the husband took up flying lessons. Not long into his training, he was involved in an accident that took his life. When I went to visit his widow and deliver the $100,000 life insurance check, she expressed her regret at not taking my advice months ago. Of course, none of us knew then that a catastrophe would soon unfold. But that was the point in trying to plan ahead.

YOUR CONCERN

Business professionals proactively plan their days, careers, meetings, marketing initiatives and more. Few executives are procrastinators at work, but many fly by the seat of their pants at home.

By the time they visit a financial planner, many are wondering why they are so effective at work, but have lost control at home. Executives who prepare detailed plans to avoid financial calamity in their professional lives often believe they are immune to devastation at home. Consider the client in his 50s. Each time his financial planner says "when you die," this client interjects, "No, it's 'if you die'." Mortality can be a difficult thing to accept, even as we age. And yet, we all face the same final countdown – it's just a matter of when.

A group of American pilots during World War II were informed before a tour of duty that two-thirds of them likely would not return. Interestingly, this gloomy prediction had little impact. Most of the pilots looked at the guys on either side of them and thought, "That poor guy is never going to see his family again." Most people find it difficult to imagine that something bad could happen to them.

You may be smart. But that doesn't mean it's easy for you to see what tomorrow might look like. For example, talking about the need to save for the future sounds great. But personally observing the impact of not saving is far more powerful and life-changing. Knowing that you need to protect your family from risks is one thing. Actually seeing the financial outcome is far different.

How often have you thought, "I really need to have my investments, will and insurance reviewed?" Yet another year goes by, and you don't get it done. Is it really that you don't have time? Or do you simply want to believe that bad things happening to other people won't happen to you?

THE SOLUTION

It isn't a matter of *if,* but *when,* tragedy will strike. To reduce the recovery time after one of life's inevitable, destructive blows, prepare a sound personal financial plan – today.

The Prosprus process:

- makes it graphically clear what impact reactive planning will have on your life

- helps you emotionally identify with the financial impact of a tragedy

- motivates you to make changes that can avert financial devastation

KEY QUESTIONS

1. Have you determined the impact of a premature death or disability on your family's financial well-being? Have you created a financial contingency plan to avoid unacceptable outcomes?

2. Have you been putting off financial planning because bad things happen to "other" people?

3. Have you extensively planned for the things that can go wrong, as well as the things that can go right?

SPOUSAL UNITY

"Nothing can be more absurd than the practice that prevails in our country of men and women not following the same pursuits with all their strengths and with one mind, for thus, the state instead of being whole is reduced to half."
PLATO

THE DILEMMA

It doesn't matter who brings home the bacon or who brings home *more* bacon if you and your spouse can't agree on what to do *with* the bacon.

Case in Point

We met with a couple who had enjoyed a great lifestyle for many years. The husband had earned a substantial six-figure salary as an executive, made sound investments and, if the couple could substantially reduce one particular hobby, the husband would be able to achieve financial independence by the time he was 60.

The man and his wife participated in a financial planning session with our team. We revealed that at their current cash-flow consumption, the couple's accumulated assets would be depleted by the time the husband turned 76. Making matters more tenuous, both the husband and wife had parents still alive in their mid-80s, indicating they were genetically predisposed to outlive their future funds. Both the husband and wife immediately understood the situation, and both were committed to improvement.

It was obvious to everyone that the situation was unacceptable. We ran several scenarios to determine how to create long-term financial independence for the couple. They needed to annually redirect $150,000 of spending into savings from their current age of 45 until their retirement age of 60.

This wasn't a newly created state of affairs, and it had been addressed in previous sessions with other financial planners. So what made the situation abundantly obvious this time to both the husband and wife? Prosprus. Previous attempts at planning had produced pages and pages of mind-numbing spreadsheets that said basically the same thing. But seeing several potential outcomes, presented graphically in real-time, helped our clients to truly identify with the changes that needed to take place.

Fast-forward to our next meeting. After discussion, the couple agreed to rein in an expensive hobby. By significantly reducing the expenses associated with this hobby, the couple could invest an additional $150,000 every year. We later learned that seeing the projected outcomes of both scenarios spurred this quick decision.

YOUR CONCERN

Regardless of who brings in the money, spouses need a shared financial vision. To get on track, both spouses must take action. And this action is prompted when both recognize that, to maintain their lifestyle, they will either run out of money or work far longer than they desire.

Even the most successful financial planners can only do so much. Planners can keep a couple focused and guide them through confusion. But with Prosprus, a couple can create realistic, shared expectations.

Typically, knowledge about household finances is not centrally located in one spouse. One spouse may keep track of investments and insurance, while the other handles day-to-day expenses. Therefore, it is essential that both be involved in the planning process, from beginning to end. Both spouses must have their interests represented, and it is easier to make sure all desires and objectives are accounted for if both spouses are involved.

Consider a client whose wife was unable to attend the initial fact-finding meeting. The husband answered every question and was certain he had not omitted any material facts. His wife attended the next meeting and began offering her insight immediately. Toward the end of the meeting, she asked a probing question about the lifestyle expenses her husband had reported. She did not see the line item for her husband's expensive car purchases. The husband then admitted, with a sheepish grin, that he had excluded this additional expense. A change to the plan graphically presented the impact of this new information. Unfortunately for the husband, this additional expense cratered the couple's financial independence. A picture truly is worth a thousand words. The look on the wife's face as she turned to her husband had to be worth several thousand words.

Nearly every day, financial planners encounter situations in which a husband and wife have markedly different expectations for the future. The husband is concerned about how to fund the children's education accounts, while the wife is concerned about where she and the kids will be should the husband die prematurely. Or the husband wants to use any cash flow surpluses to save for retirement, while the wife prefers to use the money for home improvements. Or the wife wants to save for the future, but the husband wants a new Mercedes. Neither the husband nor the wife is necessarily wrong in any of these scenarios. What both need is a plan that will make sure the most important objectives are accomplished. This will assure unity in whatever decisions are made in the future.

Financial planning is ultimately about achieving balance in your financial life. It is about making sure that you enjoy the present, but not at the expense of the future.

THE SOLUTION

Unity between spouses is absolutely essential to a successful financial plan. If only one spouse is committed to the process, then the planning exercise could be a fruitless endeavor. Leaving your biases at home and coming with a clean slate will produce far better results than using the planning process to "show" your spouse that he or she is the real problem.

The Prosprus process:

- results in the development of one coordinated plan that represents the needs and objectives of both spouses

- impartially details what changes will bring unity back to the financial household

- creates a system that demonstrates, not dictates, whether spending and savings patterns are adequate

KEY QUESTIONS

1. Does the topic of household expenses cause friction between you and your spouse?

2. Does it seem as though you and your spouse just don't share the same "vision" of the future?

3. Have you ever allowed a financial planner to create a plan that you and your spouse were committed to seeing through to completion?

4. Is your spouse an active participant in all of your financial decisions?

CHAPTER 7

SOMETIMES YOU DON'T KNOW WHAT YOU DON'T KNOW

"Not ignorance, but ignorance of ignorance, is the death of knowledge."
ALFRED NORTH WHITEHEAD

THE DILEMMA

There is serious danger out there for "do-it-yourselfers" who believe that they have already taken care of everything and don't need the help or advice of experts.

Case in Point

Bill is a busy small-business owner. Like most business owners, he never has enough time to meet all the demands of home and work. One evening, Bill discovered a minor plumbing problem in one of his bathrooms at home. After unsuccessfully using a plunger to remove the clog, Bill briefly considered hiring a plumber before deciding to fix it himself.

Bill rented a power auger and attempted to remove the obstruction via the toilet. But he found no clog. So he decided the problem must be in the air vent accessible from the roof. He grabbed the power auger and a ladder and headed outside. Once on the roof, he started up the auger and placed it in the air vent to work it down through the piping. Believing that he would know when he hit the obstruction, he continued to feed the auger.

Bill's wife was near the bathroom when she heard an awful noise. The auger had worked its way through the air vent piping and had come up through the toilet and into the bathroom. Since Bill had not felt any obstruction, he kept feeding away. The tip of the auger started swirling wildly throughout the bathroom. It broke the toilet in half. It ripped the shower curtain off the wall and slung it around the bathroom. As it wildly thrashed around the room, the auger smashed into the window, breaking it to pieces.

Bill's wife yelled at him to turn the auger off, but he couldn't hear her. She ran outside, still yelling to Bill to shut down the auger. By the time he heard her, the bathroom was a wreck.

The do-it-yourself project had gone all wrong. Bill did not know that he did not know enough to operate an auger properly. Unfortunately, his new knowledge came after the unfortunate destruction of his bathroom. In the end, he not only had to call a plumber for help, but he also had to pay to have his bathroom repaired.

YOUR CONCERN

Most of us have a story like Bill's. Maybe you tried to fix your car, patch a leaking roof or diagnose a funny sound coming from your refrigerator. After spending several frustrating hours trying to be a mechanic, you started to add up the money that you "saved," only to admit that you were still going to need to hire an expert. This expert likely charged more than he or she would have because you created an additional mess. Hiring an expert from the beginning would have been a much better use of your time and resources.

Unfortunately, in some areas of life there are no do-overs. Much of financial planning falls into this area. Deciding to self-diagnose how much life insurance you need could have a devastating impact on your family. Failure to have proper estate planning documents could cost your family hundreds of thousands of dollars in unnecessary taxes. Failure to implement asset protection strategies could cost everything you have worked a lifetime to obtain.

For example, in the mid-1980s, Texas saw a serious economic recession in the real-estate industry. One day, a man went on his daily jog. Upon completing his run, he collapsed at his mailbox. The heart attack took his life. Not long after that day, his young family moved and left their home, schools and friends behind. The jogger's widow said, "I miss my husband so much *and* I am so mad at him." He had allowed his life insurance to lapse. Ironically, the very mailbox that he died next to contained the proposal for him to purchase new coverage. This husband and father did not know that he would soon die. But there is no do-over when it comes to death. We don't know the actual numbers on our personal countdown.

Just like this man, many do-it-yourselfers believe they have completed a thorough financial plan. Yet most of the time, they have simply completed a will, hired a professional to complete their tax returns and occasionally purchased investments from an advisor. These are all essential areas of financial planning, but they really just scratch the surface. Most people are not aware of the many other areas that need to be addressed.

For example, one do-it-yourself financial planner purchased a property and casualty insurance policy. But when an expert reviewed the policy, it was discovered that visitors to the client's house were not covered under his liability policy if they rode his jet skis. His family was covered, but not family friends – a huge risk. The client thought he knew everything he needed to know, but his knowledge was not as complete as he thought.

OUR SOLUTION

One problem in our financial lives is the failure to take action on things with which we know we need to deal. An equally large problem, or maybe even larger, is the failure to take action on items of which we are completely unaware. In other words – we don't know what we don't know. We often think we have enough information and have done all we need to do. However, with hindsight, we discover we did not have all the *relevant* information.

The Prosprus process:

- is designed to inform you of the key financial planning areas that impact your life

- makes certain that you have a team of specialists – not planners – available to identify issues of which you may be unaware

- maximizes your time and money by eliminating costly do-it-yourself mistakes

KEY QUESTIONS

1. Have you ever decided to do-it-yourself and later regretted it?

2. Are certain areas in life just too important to take chances with?

3. Do you really have time to adequately advise yourself in all the areas in which you currently serve as your own advisor?

CHAPTER 8

EXECUTION AND ACCOUNTABILITY

"Well done is better than well said."
BENJAMIN FRANKLIN

THE DILEMMA

You develop a business plan at work to serve as a guide for you and your team. But it is the *execution* of the plan that will create the future the plan defines. Execution is the step you've failed to take at home.

Case in Point

We secured four separate clients as a result of working with John. I would like to say we gained these clients because they saw John's life change for the better after working with us. Unfortunately, that is not the case.

We completed a plan for John. As part of the planning process, we created an implementation sheet that detailed all the actions we recommended he take. For the next two years, we tried repeatedly to get John to execute our recommendations. Each time, he told us that as soon as he finished the next big project at his company, he would get serious about the execution of his plan. It got to the point that when we called John to encourage him to take action, he began our conversation with, "I know, I know."

John never executed any of our recommendations. One morning, as he was driving to work, John, who was in his early 40s, was in an automobile accident. He died a few hours later. As we would later discover, our original recommendation list still sat on John's desk at work. The only thing missing from the list was the far right column, which provided a place to check off each item as it was completed. This column was blank.

The legacy that John left behind was a business that had no value because the owner was gone, a wife with young children who now needed to go back to work, and employees who now needed to find new careers. All of which was totally unnecessary.

As I said, we have four clients as a result of our relationship with John. The first two came to us because John told them we would make sure their lives changed positively. Even though John had not executed our plan, he recognized its value. The other two clients came to us after John's death. They wanted to make sure they avoided the tragedy through which John's family and employees had lived.

YOUR CONCERN

A plan is only as effective as the steps taken to bring it to life. Change, however, is triggered by motivation. To get that motivation, clients need a clear, visual map to their financial future.

Prosprus is the only financial planning process that enables people – especially busy executives – to see how to engineer their futures. This ensures they will be perpetually motivated to execute their plans.

Consider a skeptical client's view of Prosprus when he said, "I'm going to try this planning stuff one more time because you've said some things no one else has, but I've tried financial planning twice before with less-than-stellar results." He followed with, "I doubt your process will be any more successful than the others." Thanks to Prosprus, the outcome was very successful, and the skeptic is now one of the process' most vocal advocates.

This client will tell you that success came because his financial planners fulfilled their promises. But it is also because he did his part, and the process made it easy.

You, like most executives, are capable of taking action on your own. But as Dr. Phil likes to ask, "How's that working for you?" If you've been through planning with little to no results, chances are you got good information, good recommendations and an attractive binder. The breakdown came when you were instructed to *execute* the plan.

In delivering a speech to a group of entrepreneurs, one client said, "Five frogs are sitting on the edge of a pond. Four frogs decide to jump in. How many frogs are still sitting on the edge of the pond? Your first thought is that one frog remains. Actually all five frogs are still on the edge of the pond. Four frogs *decided* to jump in the pond, but that does not mean that they actually jumped in."

The above fable dramatizes the distinction between *deciding* to do something and actually *doing* something. The world is full of people who *decide* to do something. New Year's resolutions are a perfect example. But just a few days into a new year, how many people are actually executing the plan? In the end, it all comes down to accountability.

With Prosprus, clients are introduced to all the implementation experts they will need. If a new will is needed, they are set up with an attorney. If the investment portfolio needs to be reallocated, they are introduced to an investment advisor. If the property and casualty insurance policies need updating, they are referred to an independent agent for a second opinion. Once the client agrees, his or her financial planner drives the execution process from beginning to end. This is what separates the Prosprus approach from most other planning processes.

Finally, execution of your plan is not possible until you commit to taking action. You must decide that nothing will stop you from achieving your objectives at home, any more than you would let obstacles prevent you from achieving your goals at work.

Remember, failure to take action in financial planning will impact not only you, but also your spouse, children, grandchildren and generations to come. A legacy of successful planning will cause a ripple effect that will benefit your descendants in ways you may never even know. Just remember the clock is ticking. The countdown for success or failure has started.

THE SOLUTION

Prosprus drives accountability. When a client creates a financial plan, he or she has finished only the first half of the process. *Success* lies in the *execution* of the plan. If execution is left to the client, nine times out of 10 the client will end up no better off than before the plan was started. The client may be smarter, but he or she will not be better-off financially. Remember, smarter is not the goal. Better-off financially is the goal.

The Prosprus process:

- creates an accountability-based structure on which you and your team of advisors can agree

- helps you prioritize all your options, so you can concentrate on the ones that need to be executed

- ensures maximum efficiency by only requiring you to be available to execute the recommendations of individual experts coordinated by planning specialists

KEY QUESTIONS

1. Have you completed planning, only to drop the ball at the time of execution?

2. Did you get a checklist of items that needed to be completed at the end of your planning session?

3. Did your financial planner hold you accountable to execute the plan?

APPLYING THE PROSPRUS PRINCIPLES

The first part of this book should have convinced you that financial planning is a worthy use of your time. And by using Prosprus, a financial plan can be created with relative ease.

Now let's focus on the basics of the products you should consider using to achieve your financial planning goals, including insurance, investment tools and estate planning techniques. There are scores of books on these topics, but few are written for busy business professionals. The data in this book is synthesized to reveal the relevant information and present the options in a logical, decision-making format.

Part 2 uses quick case studies to introduce each product and presents graphs, rather than numerical columns, to illustrate meaningful applications of these products.

CHAPTER 9

GRAPH DESCRIPTIONS

As the old saying goes, a picture is worth a thousand words. More relevant to financial planning, a picture is worth thousands of numbers on a spreadsheet.

Imagine for a moment that you are visiting a plastic surgeon. You wish to determine whether you should have something done about that lump on the ridge of your nose. The doctor takes a picture of your face as it is right now, lumpy nose and all. The doctor puts that picture side-by-side with another picture showing how your nose would look after surgery. The doctor can show a wide range of variations, from a slight alteration to a major reworking of your nose. You simply sit back and decide which version fits your situation best.

Now imagine that instead of your own before-and-after photos, you are presented with a book of pictures of noses. These noses are not on a face, much less your face. It would be much harder to visualize and personalize the outcome if you were not able to observe the potential outcome applied to *your* appearance.

Finally, imagine that no matter which method described above that your doctor chose to use, she never discussed such weighty matters as cost, risks, recovery time or pain. Anyone electing to have this surgery would want answers to these questions before taking action. For example, what if correcting this minor nose problem would require you to spend all of your emergency reserve money? Would it be worth it? Maybe or maybe not, but that decision should be yours – not the doctor's.

The Prosprus financial planning process graphically displays a client's financial life as it is right now. It then creates a plan that shows where the client wants to be. This is displayed side-by-side with the current situation. The second model will require the client to make changes in his or her current plan to achieve the desired results. The financial planner then quantifies the costs to implement the desired plan by making alterations to the original plan one at a time. If the costs are too great, the planner looks for alternatives. For instance, if the annual savings required to retire by age 60 is just too high, then Prosprus graphically shows alternatives. These might include working until age 65 and/or reducing lifestyle expenses after retirement. Many times, the optimal solution is some combination of these two options, along with others not mentioned here.

Here is the bottom line: the optimal solution is not the decision of the financial planner – it's the client's decision. Prosprus simply places the client in a position to make informed decisions.

From this point on, many chapters will incorporate the graphs used to illustrate specific planning techniques. Therefore, you need an understanding of how to read the graphs.

Graph 9-1 is made up of two separate graphs which illustrate cash flow and net worth. This is a sample of what a typical plan might look like.

Graph 9-1

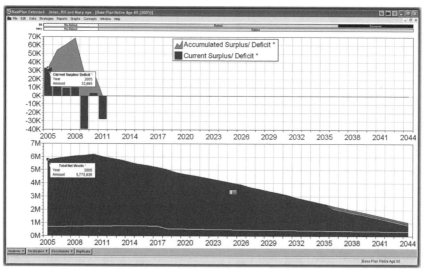

The top part of Graph 9-1 represents net cash flow. As you can see from the top of the bar, our hypothetical clients, Bill and Mary, had a cash-flow surplus of $32,865 in 2005. This means that when accounting for all household income and then subtracting all household expenses, Bill and Mary had $32,865 left over. In fact, Bill and Mary are projected to incur cash-flow surpluses through the year 2008.

The bottom part of Graph 9-1 represents the couple's total net worth in 2005: $5,775,838. The horizontal line at the bottom of the graph represents lifestyle assets. The lifestyle assets line reflects the equity in the couple's homes. Everything below the line is home equity. Everything else is included in the area above the line. This includes cash, brokerage accounts, 401(k), IRA, business interests, collectibles, land, etc.

Graph 9-1 reflects all cash flow and net worth in the "buying power" of 2005. This means that it adjusts the balances for inflation. In essence, the graph reflects what it will "feel" like, not what the balances will actually be.

Graph 9-2

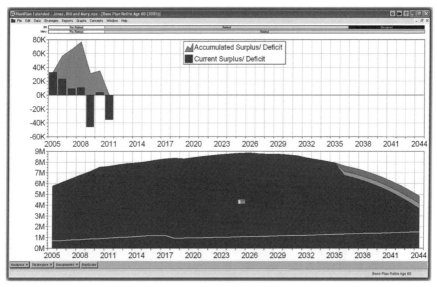

As you can see, Graph 9-2 leaves a completely different impression than Graph 9-1. In the first year, 2005, both graphs are the same. After that, the graphs start to look substantially different. Toward the end of the graphs, in 2044, there is a substantial difference between the graphs in Bill and Mary's net worth. Graph 9-2 shows a net worth of just less than $5 million. Graph 9-1 shows a net worth of a little over $1 million. This means that in the year 2044, at a four-percent inflation rate, it will take nearly $5 million to equal what we know today as $1 million.

The reality is that we live our lives according to Graph 9-1. Having a net worth of nearly $5 million at death sounds great (except the death part, of course). But if you know it is really only worth what we think of as $1 million today, do you have the same feeling? Graph 9-2 leaves the false impression that the couple's net worth is remaining stable. The account values are relatively stable, but inflation is slowly eating away at the buying power of the assets. Graph 9-2 leaves the couple with the impression that things are great and additional spending is fine. Graph 9-1 tells the couple to be very careful.

For this reason, Prosprus works almost exclusively with buying-power graphs. It sets the framework for more productive meetings. Prosprus does use nominal-dollar graphs to illustrate the potential for estate taxes at the death of the second spouse. Other than that, nominal-dollar graphs have very little usefulness.

The problem in the financial planning world is that almost all planners work from a nominal-dollar graph, such as Graph 9-2. Graph 9-2 might cause a CPA or attorney to suggest that the couple start making gifts to the children to help minimize estate taxes. But the fact is that the couple is giving away their financial independence each time they make a gift. If the couple was working from Graph 9-1, it is unlikely that they would feel very compelled to make gifts.

When working on your financial plan, insist that your financial planner illustrate what impact inflation will have on your real net worth. This information is what really matters.

The remainder of this book will use graphs very similar to the ones above. They will be illustrated in terms of buying power, unless otherwise specified.

CHAPTER 10

RETIREMENT PLANNING

Most clients complete a financial plan to make certain they are on track for retirement. But we avoid the term "retirement" because what clients really want is financial independence. Most will continue to work well into their 60s, and sometimes even into their 70s. What they really want to know is this: when can they work because they *want* to, not because they *have* to?

Financial independence means something different to each client. True financial planning attempts to get at the heart of what is most important to each individual. For one client, financial independence means having a specified amount of money that can be spent monthly during retirement. For another, it means walking away from it all at age 60, even if lifestyle expenses have to be reduced substantially. For another, financial independence means having to work harder now and earn more money so that an early life of leisure is possible. For yet another, it means investing more aggressively while young in order to achieve an earlier financial independence.

Case in Point

Financial independence was the primary concern for Doug and Becky, who were in their mid-40s. During one of our planning meetings, we spent a significant amount of time trying to specifically define what was needed to satisfy what both wanted in terms of financial independence. Early on, it became clear that leaving work at age 55 was not possible at their current level of lifestyle expenses.

We engaged Doug and Becky in a conversation about what mattered most to each of them. Doug made it very clear that he did not want to continue the stressful pace he endured as an executive of a very large company. He traveled a great deal in his position at work and wanted to spend more time with Becky. We also discovered that he would love to teach high school business classes if he were able to retire at 55. Becky wanted Doug to stop working the very long hours that had become common-place since he had become an executive. She was concerned about the long-term impact on Doug's health if he continued at the same pace into his late 50s. Becky wanted to enjoy an extended period of financial independence with her husband – not a long one by herself.

We then geared the entire financial independence modeling session around what it would take to achieve the savings to allow Doug to retire by age 55. He would then begin his second career as a teacher. Teaching full-time currently was not an option because neither Doug nor Becky was willing to reduce lifestyle expenses to a level that would allow Doug to give up his high-paying executive position. However, they were able to see that with proper attention to the ultimate goal, lots of savings and moderately reduced expenses, their goals could be achieved in time.

When thinking about financial independence, we must sort out what matters most. Once that is determined, the steps to get there should fall in to line. But everyone needs a starting point. Graph 10-1 is an example of a starting point.

Graph 10-1

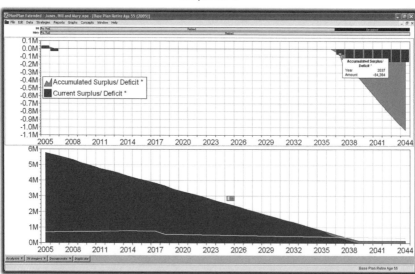

In this plan, Bill wanted to retire at age 55. But as you can see, significant cash flow deficits occur in 2037, several years before Mary reaches her life expectancy. One of the options we illustrated for Bill and Mary was to consider working until age 60, which is represented by the Graph 10-2.

Graph 10-2

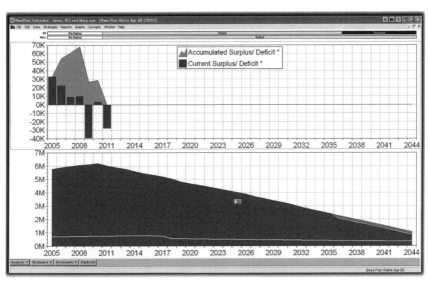

Working until age 60 eliminates the cash flow deficits at Mary's life expectancy, but it still leaves the plan way too thin at the end of their life expectancies, when their net worth has dropped from almost $6 million to around $1 million (in buying power). At the rate of decline shown, the plan will collapse if expenses are greater than anticipated or if life expectancy increases. Therefore, the next consideration was reducing retirement expenses by $20,000 per year. Graph 10-3 illustrates the results of this change.

Now their net worth at the end of their life expectancies is a more comfortable $2 million (in buying power). This level of reduction was acceptable to the couple and would still allow retirement at age 60.

Through the financial independence modeling session, Bill and Mary saw approximately 25 scenarios with multiple options that would help them achieve success. In the end, Bill and Mary took pieces of several scenarios and combined them into one plan. Without the opportunity to see multiple scenarios, they never could have arrived at a comfort level that motivated them to reduce expenses and work longer. Now they know their numbers and are executing a plan in which they believe.

Graph 10-3

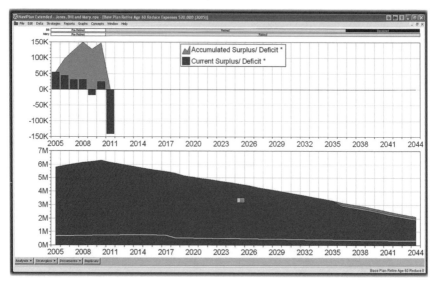

Rules of thumb for retirement – There is a rule of thumb that says it is safe to withdraw up to five percent of retirement assets each year during retirement and still enjoy a high probability of not running out of money. The problem with this rule of thumb is that it does not account for risk tolerance, retirement age or inflation.

A person who retires at age 55 and is very conservative will have a fairly high probability of running out of money if he or she withdraws five percent each year. On the other hand, someone who retires at age 70 can probably withdraw five percent and not run out of money, even if virtually all of his or her money is invested in money market accounts. Why the difference? The 55-year-old retiree will likely be retired for 30 years or more while the 70-year-old retiree will only be retired for 15 years or so. Over the years of retirement for the 70-year-old, inflation will have a far less dramatic impact than it will on the 55-year-old. The following tables illustrate this difference.

Table 10-1

Long-Term Impact of Inflation		
Scenario - Age 55		
Age	No Inflation	3% Inflation	4% Inflation
55	$5,000	$5,000	$5,000
56	$5,000	$5,150	$5,200
57	$5,000	$5,305	$5,408
58	$5,000	$5,464	$5,624
59	$5,000	$5,628	$5,849
60	$5,000	$5,796	$6,083
61	$5,000	$5,970	$6,327
62	$5,000	$6,149	$6,580
63	$5,000	$6,334	$6,843
64	$5,000	$6,524	$7,117
65	$5,000	$6,720	$7,401
66	$5,000	$6,921	$7,697
67	$5,000	$7,129	$8,005
68	$5,000	$7,343	$8,325
69	$5,000	$7,563	$8,658
70	$5,000	$7,790	$9,005
71	$5,000	$8,024	$9,365
72	$5,000	$8,264	$9,740
73	$5,000	$8,512	$10,129
74	$5,000	$8,768	$10,534
75	$5,000	$9,031	$10,956
76	$5,000	$9,301	$11,394
77	$5,000	$9,581	$11,850
78	$5,000	$9,868	$12,324
79	$5,000	$10,164	$12,817
80	$5,000	$10,469	$13,329
81	$5,000	$10,783	$13,862
82	$5,000	$11,106	$14,417
83	$5,000	$11,440	$14,994
84	$5,000	$11,783	$15,593
85	$5,000	$12,136	$16,217

Table 10-2

Long-Term Impact of Inflation			
Scenario - Age 70			
Age	No Inflation	3% Inflation	4% Inflation
70	$5,000	$5,000	$5,000
71	$5,000	$5,150	$5,200
72	$5,000	$5,305	$5,408
73	$5,000	$5,464	$5,624
74	$5,000	$5,628	$5,849
75	$5,000	$5,796	$6,083
76	$5,000	$5,970	$6,327
77	$5,000	$6,149	$6,580
78	$5,000	$6,334	$6,843
79	$5,000	$6,524	$7,117
80	$5,000	$6,720	$7,401
81	$5,000	$6,921	$7,697
82	$5,000	$7,129	$8,005
83	$5,000	$7,343	$8,325
84	$5,000	$7,563	$8,658
85	$5,000	$7,790	$9,005

As you can see from Table 10-1, by the time the 55-year-old retiree reaches age 85, his $5,000-per-month need has grown to $12,136 (assuming a three-percent inflation rate). It is very likely that a five-percent withdrawal will not be enough to meet his monthly expenses after just a few years of retirement. On the other hand, the 70-year-old retiree illustrated in Table 10-2 will likely be just fine because his need to withdraw funds from his accounts will not last nearly as long. Therefore, the long-term impact of inflation will be reduced.

Another problem with the retirement rule of thumb is that if you are assuming you will need an additional $5,000 per month above and beyond any pension and/or Social Security income, you will still need to factor in inflation. In order to withdraw the $5,000 per month, you would need a nest egg of at least $1.2 million ($1,200,000 x 5% = $60,000/12 = $5,000). But if you are a 35-year-old planning to retire at 65, it will take $12,136 to equal what you currently think of as $5,000 (assuming a three-percent inflation rate). This means that your nest egg would need to be more like $2,912,640

($2,912,640 x 5% = $145,632/12 = $12,136). Most experts do a good job informing clients how much to save at a given rate of return to have $1.2 million by the time they retire. The real issue is that at a three-percent inflation rate, you will actually need $2,912,640!

The final problem with this rule of thumb is this: if you withdraw five percent this year and only earn five percent, then the balance in your account will remain the same. Next year, you will need to withdraw 5.15 percent in order to keep pace with inflation. If you are earning only five percent, then your principal balance will drop ($1,200,000 + 5% growth = $1,260,000 x 5.15% expenses = $1,191,865). The next year, you will earn five percent on the new balance, but you will need to withdraw 5.3 percent. Each year, you will be earning less and less due to the need to withdraw from principal to meet your increasing expenses while you continue to earn less and less. You can only hope that you do not live longer than your money lasts. Needing to die young is not what we define as proactive financial planning.

Lifestyle expenses during retirement – The rule of thumb here is that retirees will only need 70 percent to 80 percent of their pre-retirement budget during retirement. Certainly some expenses (such as housing) should go down. Most retirees should plan to have their mortgages paid off before entering retirement. This would certainly result in a reduction in expenses. The problem is that there are several new expenses that increase around re-tirement age.

Health-related costs can be much higher for retirees than for those still working. One reason is that between Medicare Part B and Medigap insur-ance, expenses can be higher than the retiree experienced while working. Also, as health deteriorates, expenses rise. And the possibility of additional costs associated with long-term care can cause expenses to rise to a level that is much higher than that before retirement. Additionally, it is human nature to spend more money when more time is available. While working, most people just don't have the time to travel as much as they would like. Additional trips to visit friends and relatives will create additional expenses. Retirees have more time for other recreational activities such as golfing, boating and shop-ping as well. Extra time can translate into extra expenses.

Given the above, most retirees should plan for an expense level that is around 90 percent of their pre-retirement expenses.

To test whether a rule of thumb is accurate in a specific situation, Prosprus can be used with each client to test the outcome of multiple sce-narios. A graphic display demonstrates the long-term results of specific fi-nancial planning decisions acted upon today. In a matter of seconds, multiple scenarios can depict the outcome of various choices. True financial planning will assist a client by providing all the relevant information needed to make an informed decision. When searching for a financial planner, make certain the one you choose can model some of the infinite possibilities that can alter any financial plan.

CHAPTER 11

INVESTMENTS, RETURNS AND RISK

One of the most fundamental assumptions in any financial plan is the return used to project the future value of investment assets. Many financial plans have built-in return assumptions that are far too aggressive. Not surprisingly, these assumptions tend to project a very successful plan. A false expectation of high returns can create a devastating impact, as seen with a new client.

Case in Point

George hired a financial planner during the raging bull market of the 1990s. A financial plan was completed, but the plan used return assumptions of 10 percent on all investment assets until the end of George's and his wife's life expectancies. In 2002, after being retired for two years, George had lost almost 40 percent of his investments. To further complicate things, since he was not working, he was withdrawing money from his accounts to support his lifestyle. In essence, he was being forced to sell his assets at precisely the wrong time – at the bottom of the market.

As we reviewed George's plan, we discovered that there had not been any downward adjustment in return expectations when George was about to retire and needed to reduce the risk and volatility of his portfolio. George had assumed that his financial planner understood a realistic return assumption for his particular case.

Since the plan had confirmed that he would be able to spend the specified amount on his lifestyle expenses, George was not particularly concerned – at first. As time went by and the bear market continued, George became increasingly concerned that his situation was not as rosy as the original plan had indicated.

When George came to us, we started his financial plan from scratch. The final results revealed that George would either have to dramatically reduce his expenses or go back to work. Neither option was appealing, but implementing at least one option was necessary.

To fully explore what went wrong in this case, let's begin with some definitions.

(The following list of investments is certainly not exhaustive. It is only meant to give a basis for our discussion.)

STOCKS

Stocks, also known as *equities*, represent ownership in a company. When an investor purchases stock, he or she is claiming an ownership stake in the future direction of the company. If the company does well, the investor likely will make money. If the company does not do well, money likely will be lost.

Stocks are further categorized by the total size of the company itself, normally referred to as *capitalization*. Capitalization is determined by multiplying the stock price by the total number of outstanding shares. If this figure is greater than $5 billion, then the stock is referred to as a *large-cap stock*. If the figure is $1 billion or less, the stock is referred to as a *small-cap stock*. Finally, *mid-cap stocks* are when capitalization falls between $1 billion and $5 billion.

BONDS

A *bond* is a debt instrument issued by an organization – a company, government agency, state, city, school district, etc. When an investor purchases a bond, he or she will be paid a certain interest rate for a specified period of time until the bond matures. Bonds are generally accepted to be less risky than stocks because, in the event of the failure of the organization, bondholder claims are considered ahead of those of stockholders in the bankruptcy proceedings. This means that all bondholders must be paid in full before stockholders receive anything. As you would expect, since there is less risk with bonds than with stocks, traditionally there has been less reward. However, bonds do have interest rate risk which can have an adverse impact on the value of bonds if interest rates rise. A rising interest rate environment can cause bond values to decrease. This is commonly known as the inverse relationship between interest rates and bond prices.

Types of Bonds

The United States Government issues several types of securities. The three main instruments are bills, notes and bonds. *Bills* have maturities of one year or less. *Notes* have maturities of two years to 10 years, and *bond* maturities are more than 10 years. All three of these instruments are backed by the full faith and credit of the U.S. Government as to the timely payment of principal and interest only. This guarantee does not eliminate market risk. They are subject to federal taxes but exempt from state taxation.

Municipal bonds are issued by government entities at the state and local levels. It is common for cities, school districts and other taxing authorities to issue bonds as a means of raising capital to finance building projects, such as libraries, city halls, schools, roads, etc. The main advantage of municipal bonds is that the income is not subject to federal income taxation; however, the income may be subject to state and local taxes and, for certain investors, may be subject to the federal alternative minimum tax.

*Corporate bond*s are issued by companies as an alternative to issuing stock. Simply stated, corporate bonds are issuers' "I owe you's" and rank "senior" to both common and preferred stocks in a corporation's capital structure. As "creditors," bondholders receive priority status over the subordinate status of "owners", the corporation's stockholders. Corporate bonds are a direct obligation of the issuing corporations and, at times, are additionally secured by a lien on specific property, plant or equipment. In most instances, corporate bonds offer semiannual, fixed-interest payments and a final stated maturity date. Interest earned is taxable at both the state and federal level.

MUTUAL FUNDS

A *mutual fund* invests in a diversified portfolio of securities. People who buy shares of a mutual fund are its owners or shareholders. Their investments provide the money for a mutual fund to buy securities such as stocks and bonds. A mutual fund can make money from its securities in two ways: a security can pay dividends or interest to the fund, or a security can rise in value. A fund can also lose money and drop in value.

There are three basic types of mutual funds: stock (also called equity), bond and money market. Stock mutual funds invest primarily in shares of stock issued by U.S. or foreign companies. Bond mutual funds invest primarily in bonds. Money market mutual funds invest mainly in short-term securities issued by the U.S. government and its agencies, U.S. corporations, and state and local governments.

Mutual funds make saving and investing simple, accessible, and affordable. The advantages of mutual funds include professional management, diversification, variety, liquidity, affordability, convenience and ease of record-keeping, as well as government regulation and full-disclosure requirements.

Now that we have a basic understanding of the types of investments that make up a typical portfolio, let's discuss how these investments apply to a financial plan. Without getting into a long, analytical discussion of modern portfolio theory, the efficient frontier, alpha, beta, standard deviation, etc., let's explore what a reasonable expectation of return might be, depending on the type of investment chosen.

Table 11-1 lists the returns for various asset classes from 1925 to 2004.

Table 11-1

Annualized Returns Before Expenses	
Small-Cap Stocks	12.70%
Large-Cap Stocks	10.40%
Long-Term Government Bonds	5.40%
Treasury Bills	3.70%
Inflation	3.00%

Source: Ibbotson Associates

Small Company Stocks are represented by the fifth capitalization quintile of stocks on the NYSE for 1926-1981 and the performance of the Dimensional Fund Advisors (DFA) Small Company Fund thereafter; Large Company Stocks are represented by the S&P 500®, which is an unmanaged group of securities; Long-Term Government Bonds are represented by the 20-year U.S. Government Bond; Treasury Bills are represented by the 30-day U.S. Treasury Bill; Inflation is represented by the Consumer Price Index.

So what does this chart tell us about return assumptions within a financial plan? Well, several things. First, an investor must take into consideration the cost to invest, thereby reducing the figures in the chart above. The cost to manage a portfolio of bonds is less than the cost to manage a portfolio of large-cap stocks, which is less than the cost to manage a portfolio of small-cap stocks. For illustrative purposes, let's make the following cost assumptions (Table 11-2):

Table 11-2

Annualized Expense Assumptions	
Small-Cap Stocks	1.25%
Large-Cap Stocks	0.90%
Long-Term Government Bonds	0.40%
Treasury Bills	0.30%
Inflation	N/A

These expense assumptions certainly are not the least nor the most expensive options that are available. These assumptions are only meant to illustrate a point.

Table 11-3

Approximate Annualized Return After Expenses	
Small-Cap Stocks	11.45%
Large-Cap Stocks	9.50%
Long-Term Government Bonds	5.00%
Treasury Bills	3.40%
Inflation	3.00%

Table 11-3 shows the net return after expenses. What you can now see is that only one category has a return that is equal to or greater than 10 percent. Therefore, it is highly aggressive to assume a double-digit return in an investment forecast.

Second, even if a 10-percent rate of return is achievable, it will require that 100 percent of investment assets be invested in stocks, including the more volatile small-cap asset class. While this will always qualify as an aggressive decision, it is absolutely indefensible for someone who is nearing retirement. And the situation becomes even more absurd as the account owner nears the end of his or her life expectancy.

Third, assuming that these investments are not in tax-deferred accounts, current taxation must be taken into consideration. The five-percent, long-term government bond return will drop to 3.75 percent, assuming an average income tax rate of 25 percent (5% x (1-.25%)). This means that once inflation is taken into consideration, the real rate of return is about .75 percent (3.75%-3.0%=.75%). At a real return rate of .75 percent, it will take an incredible amount of savings or a very long time to accumulate enough money to retire. What this really means is that while a 10-percent return until the end of life expectancy is way too aggressive, placing all your money in bonds is so conservative that it will likely leave you without enough growth or income to enjoy your retirement.

The solution is to create a diversified portfolio that incorporates enough stock exposure to adequately outpace inflation, while at the same time holding enough bonds to smooth out the ups and downs of the market. All investors must find their comfort level regarding how aggressively to invest. Just remember that most people become less and less aggressive as they approach retirement. This means that 10 percent might be a reasonable assumption in the early years, but it will not be reasonable once you retire. At the same time, becoming too conservative too soon will have an equally unsettling impact on financial independence.

CHAPTER 12

LIFE INSURANCE

One thing that drives financial planners crazy is when so-called "experts" give incredibly inaccurate rules of thumb. One can only assume that these "experts" have never actually done any financial planning because the results of following their advice can be devastating. The following case study explores a real situation where going along with a rule of thumb had a very negative consequence.

Case in Point

Over the years, we have developed financial plans for several recently widowed women. In most instances, the deceased spouse was the major breadwinner of the family. Little or no planning had been done before the accident or illness that ultimately took the life of the husband. The following is an example of a real situation we encountered:

We met Debra a few months after the death of her husband. Jim had been an executive with a local company and had provided very well for his family. Jim and Debra had raised their two sons and paid for their college education. Jim was diagnosed with cancer during the time his kids were in college. He successfully beat the cancer in round one, only to have it come back a couple of years later. This time, the cancer took his life at the young age of 47. Debra was the same age.

Debra had given up a career as a teacher to be a stay-at-home mom and had not been very involved in the financial matters of the family. Jim had updated his estate planning documents before his death, but he was too ill to teach Debra how to deal with all the decisions she would face after he was gone. Fortunately, Debra had friends and family members who stepped in to assist her with some of the immediate issues she was facing. But her long-term financial independence was a different matter.

Jim carried life insurance valued at about five times his salary and had assets valued at about three times his salary. Debra's total asset base was about eight times Jim's salary. Jim had heard many times that if he had five to 10 times his salary in life insurance, then Debra would have enough of an asset base to live comfortably for the rest of her life. Believing that this rule of thumb was a good measure of how much money Debra would need in the event of his death, Jim did not buy additional life insurance before the cancer was diagnosed.

Once we began working on Debra's financial plan, it became evident that a dramatic reduction in her lifestyle would be needed. At her previous lifestyle expense level, Debra would be bankrupt within 20 years. Ultimately, we recommended a reduction in monthly expenses of about 50 percent, with the understanding that there likely would not be a very large inheritance for her sons. Debra considered going back to work, but given that she had been out of her profession for many years and teaching did not pay nearly as well as Jim's profession had, this solution would have only marginally improved the situation. It certainly would not have corrected it.

Jim and Debra lived a nice upper-middle-class lifestyle before Jim's premature death. But no matter the economic status, a reduction of 50 percent is extreme. As you review your own situation, be careful not to take rules of thumb at face value. Either test them yourself or hire a qualified financial planner to do it for you. Know the impact of your financial decisions before those decisions hurt you and your family in the future.

As the case study above illustrates, the often-repeated rule of thumb regarding how much life insurance an individual should have can be terribly inaccurate. The typical rule is to have five to 10 times salary in life insurance, but let's examine why this is far too little insurance.

Suppose you have a man who makes $100,000 a year, is married with two children, and his spouse is a stay-at-home mother. If this family is anything like most families, they spend about $6,000 per month on living expenses. The remainder of the income goes into his 401(k) and to pay income taxes. Very likely most of that $6,000 per month is for expenses that do not go away just because the husband is deceased. Most expenses (rent/mortgage payments, utilities, insurance, property taxes, college expenses, etc.) don't go down. In fact, some expenses will go up (childcare, home maintenance and repair, etc.).

For the sake of argument, let's assume that expenses do drop from $6,000 to $5,000 per month ($60,000 per year), not including college expenses of $15,000 per year for four years for two children. Once the surviving spouse receives all the assets of her deceased husband, along with the life insurance proceeds, she invests the assets in a balanced and diversified portfolio with a projected total return of seven percent. Next, let's assume an annual inflation rate of three percent, which leaves us with a real rate of return of four percent. Finally, let's assume an average tax rate of 20 percent. This should leave an after-tax real rate of return of 2.6 percent [7% - (7% x 20%) -3%]. (This is a simple formula that is not intended to be precise. It is only intended to be an approximation and to illustrate a point.)

So if the insured had as much as 10 times his salary in life insurance (the high end of the rule of thumb), he would have had $1 million worth of life insurance. We also assume he had approximately $200,000 in assets, including a home with no mortgage. It may sound like a lot, but in reality it is likely not nearly enough. Multiply the after-tax real rate of return of 2.6 percent by $1 million and you will see that the surviving spouse will only receive $26,000 per year. Since we decided that she will need $60,000 per year, she will have to start spending principal immediately. This means that in the second year, she will no longer have $1 million invested and thus will have less income generated. She will then need to spend even more principal than the year before. Unfortunately, this is a very slippery slope where you pick up speed as time goes on.

Graph 12-1 shows this slippery slope.

Graph 12-1

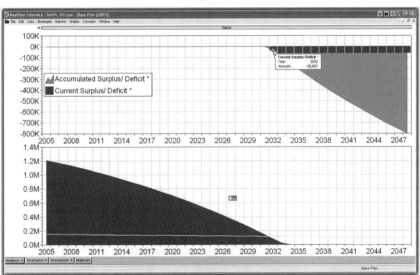

As you can see at the top part of Graph 12-1, the plan starts to run into significant cash flow deficits in the year 2032, when the survivor is only age 73. When we complete financial plans, we design them to look more like Graph 12-2. This graph assumes the client will have total assets of $2.3 million ($150,000 of which is the mortgage-free home).

Graph 12-2

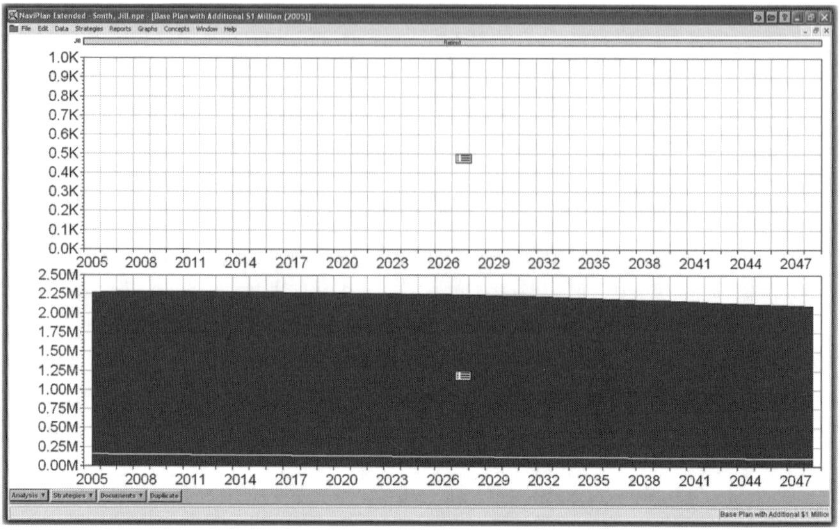

Graph 12-2 shows a plan for the client to maintain her buying power up to and beyond life expectancy.

In our examples above, we have not included Social Security payments that the surviving spouse would receive at retirement. If Social Security payments were available, then the timeframe that the $1 million could last would be lengthened. However, it would only delay the inevitable. Also, we have not included the additional costs that could be associated with college expenses, weddings, cars and insurance for children, etc. The $5,000 per month budget could prove to be inadequate. If the monthly budget turns out to be higher, then the negative consequences become even more extreme.

A quick method to determine how much your family will need in total assets is as follows:

1) Assume a moderate level of risk is acceptable, and project a seven-percent return on investments.

2) Assume an inflation rate of three percent.

3) Assume an average tax rate of 20 percent.

4) Assume results in an after-tax-and-inflation return of 2.6 percent [7 x (1- .20) – 3].

5) Assume for every $1 million worth of investment assets, you will receive $26,000 ($1,000,000 x 2.6% = $26,000).

6) Determine how much income your family will need each year (i.e. $60,000).

7) Divide #6 by $26,000 and the result is how many million dollars in investment assets you need (i.e. $60,000/$26,000 = 2.3, so $2.3 million dollars is needed).

8) Subtract any investment assets you currently have (401(k), IRAs, brokerage account, savings account, etc.) from this total.

9) The resulting figure is how much insurance you will need to buy.

Go back to our hypothetical person who earns $100,000 per year. He estimates that his family will need $60,000 per year to maintain the lifestyle to which they are accustomed. As you can see, unless he already has investment assets of $1.3 million, he is significantly underinsured. Our experience has been that anyone with assets of $1.3 million has a lifestyle of more than $60,000; therefore, the total need for insurance is higher. Exceptions to this are rare.

This is a highly simplified model that is only intended to give an approximate figure. In our financial planning practice, we use a much more involved method to calculate the exact needs of our clients and exactly how long that need will last. The main lesson to learn from this example is that the rule of thumb is a very poor measure of how much life insurance an individual should own. And why would you rely on approximations, rules of thumb or guesses when a system exists to give you precise numbers?

Now let's take a brief look at the various types of life insurance. Keep in mind that guarantees offered by life insurance are subject to the claims-paying ability of the issuing insurance company.

TERM

Term life insurance is designed to provide protection for a limited period of time. The face amount is only paid if the insured person dies during the period of coverage. This type of coverage is not unlike homeowner's and automobile insurance, conceptually. If you allow your auto insurance policy to expire and then have a wreck, the insurance company will not be obligated to pay any benefits. With a term life insurance policy, if the policy expires and the insured dies, then no benefit will be paid.

Term insurance can be purchased for premiums that are guaranteed for one, five, 10, 15, 20 and even 30 years. The longer the guarantee period, the higher the premium. For example, a 30-year premium guarantee will cost much more than a one-year premium guarantee. Term insurance does not build any cash value, so at the end of the guarantee term, the policy normally lapses, and the insured and the insurance company go their separate ways.

Term insurance is most appropriate for needs that have a specific timeframe. For example, a business owner takes out a bank loan that has a 10-year amortization schedule. The bank likely will require that the business owner take out a policy that matches the amount owed to the bank. Likely, the most affordable option for the business owner is to purchase a policy that matches the term of the loan – in this case, a 10-year policy – so that the coverage expires when it is no longer needed for the loan.

Term insurance is also appropriate for those with limited funds to purchase life insurance. Young families are often the ones who have the greatest need and the least ability to pay for the coverage. A husband and wife who are in the beginning of their careers and have two children likely will not have a lot of money left over after paying the bills. Consequently, the most affordable option to obtain a meaningful amount of life insurance coverage is to purchase term. It would likely be advisable for such a couple to purchase a 20-year term policy so that affordable coverage is guaranteed until the children are grown and possibly have even completed college.

UNIVERSAL LIFE

Universal life (UL) insurance was first introduced in 1979. Since that time, there have been more and more variations on the original idea. Universal life is a flexible policy that allows the policyholder to adjust both the premiums paid and the death benefit, within certain limits. It works well for those who have unsteady cash flow. In years when cash flow is good, a policyholder can pay more. In tight cash-flow years, maybe no premium at all is appropriate.

Cash values of universal life policies have the potential to build at interest rates as determined by the issuing insurance company. As time goes by, the death benefit remains constant, while the total amount at risk for the insurance company drops. This is due to the fact that the cash value should be continually rising. For example, early on, if the insurance company issues a $1 million policy and the insured dies, the insurance company is out almost the entire policy amount. But many years later, when the cash value of the policy is worth $200,000, the insurance company is only at risk for $800,000. This reduction in risk for the insurance company works to the benefit of the policyholder because he or she will only incur mortality charges for the remaining amount for which the insurance company is at risk. It is possible to receive both the cash value and the death benefit, but it means that the policy will have to cover the mortality charges for $1 million for the life of the contract. Ultimately, this will mean that the cash value will not grow at as fast a pace as otherwise could be expected.

The drawback to a universal life policy is that the policyholder shoulders the mortality and investment risk. If life expectancy decreases (which has not happened in a very long time, but certainly could), the additional costs to the insurance company would be passed along to the policyholder. If the rate of return was less than originally illustrated, additional premiums would be required. Of course, the opposite is true as well. If returns were greater than illustrated, premiums could be reduced.

One of the latest variations to universal life is the creation of a rider that guarantees the death benefit no matter what happens to the underlying cash value. This policy is sort of a hybrid between whole life and universal life. Under this arrangement, if the policyholder pays the required premium for the required amount of time, the insurance company will guarantee the death benefit no matter what happens to the cash value. Without this rider, if the cash value drops to zero, then the policy lapses and no death benefit is paid. Usually this rider increases the premiums of the policy, but it will still be more affordable than whole life insurance. This type of policy is excellent for estate planning solutions where the death benefit is all that matters, and cash value is not relevant. It carries the certainty of performance of whole life, without the cost.

Another variation of universal life is *variable universal life* (VUL). A VUL policy operates similarly to universal life except that the underlying cash value is invested in subaccounts. The policy owner can choose among several subaccounts, each of which has its own investment strategy and invests the money in stocks, bonds, money market or other securities in order to build the policy's cash value. However, because the performance of these investments is not guaranteed, there is an element of risk. This risk is shouldered entirely by the policyholder, and if returns do not meet expectations, the policy can lapse, leaving the policyholder without coverage. The performance of the subaccounts can vary greatly based upon the performance of the stock and bond markets. A VUL policy should only be purchased if the owner has a high enough tolerance and a time horizon that will allow for the inevitable ups and downs of the markets.

WHOLE LIFE

Whole life, also known as ordinary life, is, as the name implies, insurance that will last for the policyholder's whole life. The typical policy charges a premium that will be paid for the entire life of the policy. The insurance company shoulders all the risk of the performance of the investments. As long as the premium is paid until the death of the policyholder, the death benefit will be paid. All the risk of decreased mortality and poor investment performance is the responsibility of the insurance company. Of course, as you might expect, with decreased risk to the policyholder comes increased cost. Therefore, whole life is usually the most expensive type of insurance policy to purchase.

SURVIVORSHIP

Survivorship policies, also known as "second to die," can be in virtually any form (whole, UL, VUL). The idea is to provide funds that are only needed at the death of the second spouse. The most common application of this type of insurance is in estate planning. Since estate taxes are only due at the death of the second spouse, the need for liquidity to pay those taxes only surfaces at the time of the second death. From an actuarial point of view, insurance companies know that one of the two people insured is more likely to live to life expectancy or beyond than one person alone. Therefore, the premium costs are reduced to reflect the reduced risk to the insurance company. This is a very efficient tool to use to solve the liquidity problem that most taxable estates face at the second death.

CHAPTER 13

LONG-TERM CARE INSURANCE – WHAT YOU NEED TO KNOW

Perhaps one of the most discussed financial products these days is long-term-care insurance. It seems as if most of the baby boomers are considering a long-term are policy since they have confronted high-cost care for their parents or grandparents.

Clients fall into two groups on long-term care issues: those who have dealt with the financial and emotional difficulties of a sick parent, grandparent or spouse, and those who will.

The following case study is a typical situation.

Case in Point

Stephen and Julie, recent clients, engaged us to complete a financial plan. During our fact-finding process, we learned that the couple was currently spending approximately $70,000 per year to provide in-home care for Julie's elderly mother, who was suffering from Alzheimer's disease. As you might imagine, this expense was creating a huge problem for Stephen and Julie as they prepared for their own retirement.

During our strategy meeting, we discussed the problem this enormous expense was creating and how it was minimizing the possibility that they would ever achieve financial independence. We discussed at length what the options were for trying to eliminate, share or reduce the burden of this expense. Julie made it clear that she was not, at that time, willing to place her mother in a nursing home, and no one else in her family was in a financial position to assist with the expenses associated with her mother's care. Stephen said that we would have to find a way to make the financial plan work with the expenses for his mother-in-law included.

We continued the strategy meeting with the expenses included.

Over the next hour, Stephen and Julie began to realize that they simply could not afford to continue to pay the $70,000 per year without making drastic reductions in their own lifestyle expenses. And even after the reduction, there would not be nearly enough money to provide long-term care for themselves.

At this point, Julie informed us that there was a "facility-only" long-term care policy on her mother. A facility-only policy is one that will provide care for the policyholder only if he or she is in a nursing home or assisted-living facility. It will not cover expenses for care received at home. Julie was just not emotionally ready to send her mother to a nursing home. We ultimately recommended that she reconsider this decision now that she fully understood the impact of continuing to pay the expense herself.

As the case study illustrates, long-term care expenses can create significant financial and emotional stress. Therefore, we discuss this issue with all of our clients no matter what their age. Most of our clients have heard that purchasing long-term care insurance is something that they should give strong consideration to once they are 60 years old or so. We believe that this is a very important topic that should be dealt with at a much younger age.

As with most types of insurance, there is a risk in waiting to purchase a long-term care policy. If your health declines, the price of the policy will go up. If your health declines significantly, you might be unable to purchase a policy at all, or it will be offered at a price that is just too high to be affordable.

As you age, a policy will cost more simply because you are older; therefore, waiting can become costly. In contrast, you could purchase a policy and pay for it for years, only to die suddenly or die within the waiting period you have chosen. You will have paid a significant amount in premiums and received nothing in return.

To determine the potential future cost of receiving long-term care, we created the following chart that predicts how much care might cost at any given age based upon an assumed five percent inflation rate. The benefit amount is based upon the cost per day ($200) in the Dallas/Ft. Worth metroplex for an individual room (no roommate) in a nice nursing home, multiplied by 365 days. The total annual cost would be $73,000. Simple inflation is obvious. You will receive exactly the amount you purchased whether you need care this year or 10, 20 or 30 years from now. Simple inflation increases the original benefit by five percent each year. Compound inflation increases the benefit by five percent, based on the most recently computed figure. Over time, compound inflation will significantly outpace simple inflation. Table 13-1 illustrates this more clearly.

Table 13-1

LONG-TERM CARE INFLATION ANALYSIS			
Age	Cost with No Inflation($)	Cost with Simple Inflation($)	Cost with Compound Inflation ($)
50	73,000	73,000	73,000
51	73,000	76,650	76,650
52	73,000	80,300	80,483
53	73,000	83,950	84,507
54	73,000	87,600	88,732
55	73,000	91,250	93,169
56	73,000	94,900	97,827
57	73,000	98,550	102,718
58	73,000	102,200	107,854
59	73,000	105,850	113,247
60	73,000	109,500	118,909
61	73,000	113,150	124,855
62	73,000	116,800	131,098
63	73,000	120,450	137,652
64	73,000	124,100	144,535
65	73,000	127,750	151,762
66	73,000	131,400	159,350
67	73,000	135,050	167,317
68	73,000	138,700	175,683
69	73,000	142,350	184,467
70	73,000	146,000	193,691
71	73,000	149,650	203,375
72	73,000	153,300	213,544
73	73,000	156,950	224,221
74	73,000	160,600	235,432
75	73,000	164,250	247,204
76	73,000	167,900	259,564
77	73,000	171,550	272,542
78	73,000	175,200	286,169
79	73,000	178,850	300,478
80	73,000	182,500	315,502
81	73,000	186,150	331,277
82	73,000	189,800	347,841
83	73,000	193,450	365,233
84	73,000	197,100	383,494
85	73,000	200,750	402,669
	$2,628,000	$4,927,500	$6,996,051

ASSUMPTIONS			
Current Age	50	Inflation Figure	5.0%
Benefit Amount	$200	Mortality Age	85

As you can see from the chart, the cost of receiving $73,000 of long-term care for someone who is 50 years old today will rise to $402,669 by the time he or she is 85. This is a daunting number. Few people will have enough assets to withstand this long-term expense.

We believe the decision to purchase a long-term care policy should be made within the context of a complete financial plan. Once you have determined that you are on track to achieve financial independence, you should insert an additional expense for long-term care and test your financial models again to see if your financial independence can withstand an extended long-term care stay for either you or your spouse. If the model can't withstand the additional expense, then purchasing a long-term care policy should be given strong consideration.

Graph 13-1 illustrates a client's financial independence (in nominal dollars) without the additional cost of long-term care expenses. As you can see, if things go exactly as planned, this client will have adequate assets available to fund retirement.

Graph 13-1

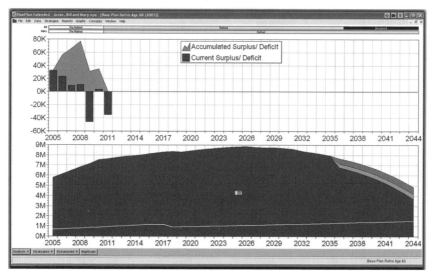

Graph 13-2 illustrates the impact (in nominal dollars) of having the additional expense of long-term care for the final five years of the husband's life. This is illustrated as an additional expense of $73,000 in today's dollars inflating at an annual rate of five percent until he turns age 80 (approximately

Graph 13-2

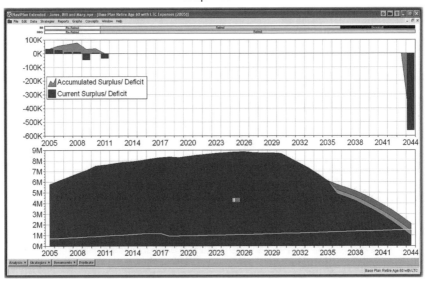

26 years). In many circumstances, one spouse needing long-term care can actually be as bad financially as if both spouses needed to receive long-term care. The reason is that if only one spouse is receiving care, the other spouse will still have the normal expenses associated with retirement. He or she will still have a home to maintain, insurance premiums, automobile expenses, utilities, groceries, etc.

As you can see, toward the end of the plan, the client would start to run cash-flow deficits because the husband's long-term care expenses would be too great a drain on the plan.

A critic would say that the odds of needing five years of long-term care is unlikely, since the average stay in a nursing home is somewhere around two to three years. That critic is right, but insurance should only be purchased to cover very large or catastrophic losses. Purchasing insurance based solely on the probability of usage shows a fundamental misunderstanding of insurance. Insurance is designed to help the policyholder avoid catastrophic losses, not average ones. This means that the client needs to give serious consideration to purchasing long-term care insurance. Of course, the decision to purchase insurance will have a negative impact on the plan described in Graph 13-1. Therefore, we always go back to model the impact on the financial independence graph.

Graph 13-3

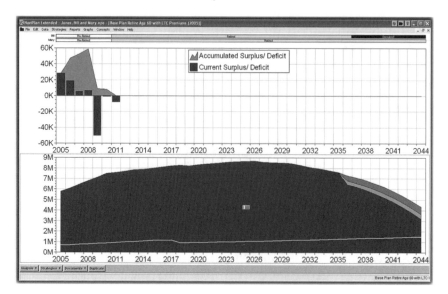

Graph 13-3 illustrates the impact (in nominal dollars) of purchasing a long-term care policy for $4,500 per year. The pricing for this policy includes coverage for both spouses for $200 per day, compound inflation and indemnity coverage. It also includes coverage for both spouses to receive care in their home, rather than having to receive care in a nursing home or assisted-living facility.

Clearly, the additional expense has a negative impact on the plan. The real question is whether the impact is significant enough to jeopardize financial independence. In this case, it is not. Therefore, the decision boils down to what we call "big mistake versus little mistake".

The "big mistake" is if you do not have a long-term care policy and end up needing care for an extended period (as in Graph 13-2). The "little mistake" is if you purchase a policy that you never use (Graph 13-3). The impact of the "big mistake" is bankruptcy and leaving your spouse without the funds to care for himself or herself. The impact of the "little mistake" is that you purchase a policy you never end up needing, and that money could have been spent on something more enjoyable than insurance premiums. Given the choice between the two possible outcomes, most people opt for the "little mistake".

Once you have determined whether long-term care makes sense in your case, there are still several matters to consider. The main thing that should never be compromised when purchasing long-term care insurance is the quality of the insurance company itself. You should only consider an insurance company that has extremely strong financials.

Life insurance companies have a long history with actuarial statistics that tell them very accurately what the probability is that an individual will die in any given year. In a group of say 10,000 individuals, insurance companies don't know who will die, but they do have a good idea how many will die during the year. The actuarial tables used by insurance companies were created over many years and are based upon the actual age of death for many, many people.

Long-term care presents a more difficult actuarial estimate. We don't have the same amount of data, and the triggering event for usage is a little less certain. Life insurance proceeds are triggered at death. Death is precise. You either are alive or you are not. Long-term care needs are less precise. What disables one person might not disable another. What one doctor considers debilitating enough to trigger long-term care benefits might not be considered so by another doctor.

What insurance companies don't know is how many people suffered in silence who might have sought care (and been qualified to receive it) if they had owned a long-term care policy. Insurance companies have a good estimate of the number of people who entered nursing homes or assisted living facilities, or received care at home. But how many people never received those types of care because they stayed with family members? Now consider whether these people would have cashed in on their long-term care policies if they had been paying for policies for many years. Of course they would.

As millions and millions of baby boomers begin to reach the traditional ages at which long-term care needs are highest, the drain on insurance companies could become a problem. All of these policyholders could be cashing in at around the same time. This could create financial pressure on the insurance companies, and in response, they will increase premiums on all those policyholders who are still paying premiums.

Long-term care policies can be purchased based upon premiums that continue for life or for a finite period of time. Most of our clients who purchase long-term care policies opt for the accelerated payment plans offered by "10-pay" contracts. A 10-pay contract allows the policy to be paid-up at the end of 10 years. Currently, long-term care contracts are written such that the insurance company has the right to increase premiums at any time, as long as premiums are still being paid. What this means is that if you elect to purchase a 10-pay contract, then the insurance company only has the right to increase your premium during the 10 years that you are actually paying premiums. After the 10 years, your contract is paid-in-full and the insurance company can't ask for additional premiums. Not all insurance company contracts operate this way. Make certain you understand the specifics of a contract before purchasing one.

If you elect to purchase a lifetime-pay contract, then the insurance company can, and likely will, increase your premiums. Insurance companies can't single you out individually and increase your premiums. Premiums can only be increased based upon an entire class of policyholders.

As usage of long-term care increases, the likelihood of premium increases will rise dramatically. If an insurance company raises premiums, the healthiest policyholders might choose to cancel their policies and purchase new ones from different companies that have not opted for premium increases. Unfortunately, policyholders whose health has declined, but not enough to trigger benefits, will not be able to switch insurance companies. This will leave only the sickest policyholders in the plan. When additional members of this group qualify for care, the insurance company will be forced to raise premiums again. At some point, the premium increases could get so high that some policyholders will be forced to cancel their policies. This is the primary reason we prefer limited-pay contracts. If you have completed your 10 annual payments on your 10-pay contract, then the insurance company can't ask you for more money.

Think about the cost of a 10-pay contract like this: if you had the opportunity to go back to the early 1990s (assuming you had the cash available), would you take the opportunity to 10-pay your health insurance premiums? Everyone knows the inflation rate for health insurance premiums has skyrocketed over the past decade and shows no signs of slowing down any time soon. If you had been able, and the insurance company had been willing, wouldn't it have been the deal of a lifetime to have pre-paid future premiums? Long-term care will probably not be quite that dramatic, but if it is 25 percent as dramatic as traditional health insurance rates, then a 10-pay contract will be a great deal.

We believe long-term care insurance should be considered even for those who could clearly afford to pay for the expense of long-term care. It is not a right-and-wrong issue. It is just a different way of viewing wealth. Many of our clients own homes without a mortgage. These same clients also have liquid assets of many times the value of their homes and their contents. None of them has determined that it would be wise to cancel their homeowner's insurance policy. Why? Because all of them worked very hard to accumulate the wealth that they have, and they believe it makes sense to insure their homes so that they do not have to set aside enough assets to replace their homes should disaster occur. They do not view having paid homeowner's insurance premiums as a waste of money just because their homes did not burn down. They just view the premium as the necessary cost to free up their other assets for better use.

Regardless of whether you purchase a 10-pay or a lifetime-pay contract, you should only consider purchasing your policy from a very highly-rated insurance company. If any of the potential events described above was to come to pass, you would need to be insured by an insurance company that is very, very secure. This is not the type of product that should be purchased based upon price alone. The financial stability of the company is paramount. The history of rate increases on any of the insurance company's products should be considered. If the insurance company has a history of raising premiums on any of its products, proceed with caution. There have been several companies that have recently increased premiums on current long-term care policyholders by as much as 50 percent. This is the kind of premium increase that will be very difficult to absorb during retirement. There are several rating services that independently determine the strength of insurance companies. The best-known of the rating services is probably the A.M. Best Company (www.ambest.com).

CHAPTER 14

EDUCATING THE CHILDREN

Most people agree that saving to pay for their children's college education is important. Virtually everyone agrees that it is vital to save early and often for retirement. But what should the priority be if there is not enough to fund both?

Case in Point

Keith and Kathy engaged us to complete a financial plan. As a physician, Keith had been through years and years of schooling and placed a very high premium on his children's education. Through our fact-finding process, it became clear that educating the children was one of his top priorities. At the time, he was paying a significant amount of money to send the children to exclusive private schools. Additionally, he wanted to set aside enough money to send his three children to an Ivy League college. He felt it was important to be prepared to pay for graduate school as well.

Keith earned a very good living as a physician, but the trappings of success meant that it would be very hard to accomplish all of his goals. He felt it was important to live in the right type of neighborhood, drive the type of car a successful doctor would drive, join the right country club, etc. After analyzing all the information that impacted how much Keith and Kathy could afford to save, it became clear that they could not afford to send the kids to such exclusive and expensive schools and still fund their own retirement without a significant change in lifestyle. This presented a dilemma that was not easy for them to reconcile. Ultimately, they had to decide what was more important: their own financial independence at the lifestyle they desired or their children's Ivy League education.

We explored multiple possibilities, but in the end it came down to priorities.

Saving for college for children is extremely important, but securing your own financial independence first is more important. There are other ways to pay for college. Students can get loans, grants and scholarships, or they can go to a less expensive school. There are organizations that will assist students in figuring out how to accomplish an educational goal. No one is interested in your financial independence except you. (Actually, there are people who are interested in your financial independence besides you – your children.) If your children get a great Ivy League education but then have to support you during retirement, they will be unable to fund their own retirement or their children's education. On the other hand, if you have saved enough money for retirement, your children will be very thankful. The children will find a way to make it through college. They may not appreciate it at the time, but they will be thankful that they do not have to worry about your retirement as they prepare for their own.

This is not to say you should not be saving for college for your children. You absolutely should. The following is a brief discussion of some of the choices you have, along with the benefits of each.

529 PLANS

Each 529 plan is sponsored by a state. All 50 states have their own plans. The plans originally were created to defer taxes on investments that were set aside to pay for college education expenses. But with the 2001 tax law, withdrawals are now free of federal taxes, as long as the proceeds are used to pay for college expenses. (Tax-free treatment will expire 12/31/2010 unless extended by law.) If withdrawals are made to pay for anything other than college, then income taxes will be due along with a 10-percent penalty on any growth.

Each plan is a little different, but most plans have pre-set model portfolios of investments that are designed to be conservative, aggressive or somewhere in between. Some plans will allow the investments to be changed periodically. (Recent tax law has loosened the rules on switching between investments.) Be certain that the plan you choose has an investment-allocation strategy with which you are comfortable.

State tax breaks are different from state to state. 529 plans are exempt from federal taxes, but not necessarily from state income taxes. Some states do not exempt from state income taxes the gains in a 529 plan unless you are invested in the 529 plan from that state. Other states will allow a deduction from state income taxes for any amounts contributed to a 529 plan from that state. Most set a cap on the deduction, but even a partial deduction must be considered a bonus for that state's plan.

Always check the fees before signing up for a 529 plan. Some plans have fees that are much higher than others. Fees can include an enrollment charge, maintenance fees and fees associated with managing the investments themselves. High-expense plans will create a drag on performance that will ultimately lead to a much smaller account balance than would have otherwise been experienced.

Finally, 529 plans can count against the student when applying for financial aid. But there are ways to deal with this possibility, such as having a grandparent own the account. A grandparent owning the account should keep the assets from counting in the formula of assets available to the student, but check first because the rules are complicated and filled with exceptions. Even this strategy likely will not keep the distributions out of the formula for the year in which they are received.

PREPAID TUITION PLANS

With prepaid tuition plans, the account owner pays tomorrow's tuition costs at today's prices. The weakness of this type of plan is that normally the tuition guarantee is only good if the child attends an in-state college. If an out-of-state college is chosen, then the balance is based upon the performance of the underlying investment, which may or may not equal the cost of sending the child to college. Finally, the account will definitely count against the child when applying for financial aid.

COVERDELL ACCOUNTS

Coverdell accounts, formerly known as Education IRAs, have several similarities to 529 plans. But one of the main differences is that the Coverdell account has an annual contribution limit of $2,000. This makes it only marginally useful as an accumulation vehicle because it just can't be funded with enough money to pay for college. It also has income phase-out limitations ($95,000 to $110,000 for single filers and $190,000 to $220,000 for married filing jointly) that restrict those at the upper income levels from participating. When a single taxpayer reaches an income of $95,000, the amount that can be contributed to a Coverdell account is gradually reduced until it arrives at zero once income reaches $110,000. The same applies for a married couple filing jointly from income of $190,000 to $220,000. Investment options are much more open for Coverdell accounts than for 529 plans. The account can be allocated among a variety of investments and rebalanced or altered as often as you wish.

Withdrawals are tax-free as long as they are used for education expenses. Withdrawals are also allowed for pre-college expenses such as private-school tuition. However, all withdrawals must be taken by the time the child is age

30; otherwise, the account must be liquidated and tax must be paid on the gains, along with a 10-percent penalty.

One large drawback to Coverdell accounts is that at some point the child will control the account. He or she may or may not use the money to pay for college. Mom and dad will have no say, nor can they take the money back. This could be a serious problem if the child makes poor choices upon entering adulthood.

UGMA/UTMA

Uniform Gift to Minors Act/Uniform Transfer to Minors Act accounts were created to allow minors to own assets without having to go to the trouble and expense of hiring an attorney to create a trust. The rules that govern these accounts are established by each state.

These accounts do not get much attention anymore. They were once extensively used as a way to move the tax consequences of savings from the parents to the children. For the child, in 2005, the first $800 of unearned income is not taxed at all. The second $800 is taxed at the child's rate (normally lower than the rate of the parents). Unearned income over $1,600 is taxed at the highest marginal rate of the parent. This type of taxation had positive implications for college savings accounts when compared to saving the money in a parent's name. However, with the creation of the 529 plan, these types of accounts are much less desirable.

The main drawback to UGMA/UTMA accounts is that somewhere between the age of 18 and 21 (depending on state law), the control of the account is turned over to the child. There is no penalty for not using the money for education expenses, and there is nothing to stop a child from spending the money on an expensive sports car or traveling through Europe for as long as the money will last.

There are other ways to pay for college, but these are the most popular types of accounts. This is not meant to be an exhaustive list, but rather a brief discussion on the primary options available. There are many ways to receive financial aid to fund your child's college tuition that should be explored long before the child starts college.

CHAPTER 15

ESTATE PLANNING

It is crucial to have a current will in place in the event of death. Yet most people do not have one. When the subject of estate planning comes up in the financial planning process, most clients who do not have wills hang their heads and say that they have not taken the time to deal with this very important issue. Even with those who have taken the initiative to complete wills, it is not uncommon to find that the wills are so outdated that they do not reflect what the clients would want to have happen now. Other times, in their haste, attorneys can make mistakes that would have an enormous impact on the desired estate plans.

Case in Point

James and Amanda had recently sold their business and were entering a much-deserved retirement. They engaged us to complete a financial plan that addressed their entire financial life. Part of our analysis involved a review of the estate planning documents that were currently in place.

After reviewing James' and Amanda's wills and associated trusts, we discovered a huge problem. This was a second marriage for Amanda. She had three children from a prior marriage. James did not have children. After we discussed the couple's situation with their attorney, the following structure was agreed upon: in the event of either of their deaths, the estate would be separated into two parts. One part would be placed into a trust for the benefit of the surviving spouse. The other would continue to be owned personally by the surviving spouse.

If James were to predecease Amanda, his half of the estate would be placed into the trust and would be available to Amanda until her death. At her death, the

> *assets would pass to James' brother. If Amanda were to predecease James, her half of the estate would be placed into the trust and would be available to James until his death. At his death, the assets would pass to Amanda's children.*
>
> *The problem that we discovered was this: the section of the trust that spelled out exactly what would happen in the event of a death had been incorrectly written. Ultimately, the final beneficiary of the trust if James died first would end up being Amanda's children. If Amanda died first, her ultimate beneficiary was James' brother. In the end, the trust had created a lottery. The first spouse to die would disinherit his or her intended beneficiaries. Amanda's children would end up with nothing if she died first, or James' brother would receive nothing if James died first.*

This example is one where the client had paid a good attorney a fair price to complete an estate plan, and a mistake had been made. But every day we meet people who make the greater mistake of not having an estate plan in place at all. There are major consequences to not having made certain decisions before death. Who will raise the children if both parents are gone? Who will manage the money for the benefit of the children? At what age should the children be allowed to have the money outright? Do you need to make provisions for a child with special needs? Have you elected to use a credit shelter trust in your estate plan? Each of these questions and many others must be answered in a properly drafted estate plan.

Part of the reason many people fail to create an estate plan is a lack of understanding of all the terminology involved. The following list should assist in a basic understanding of estate planning documents.

WILL

When a person dies (decedent) without a will, the assets will pass according to the laws of intestacy (dying without a will) of the state in which he or she lived. The state will step in and assume responsibility for how the estate will be distributed. These laws may or may not reflect the way the decedent actually wanted his or her assets dispersed. When a will is in place, the decedent can make specific gifts to anyone, including charities. However, the laws of intestacy do not allow for specific gifts.

A will also designates an executor who is given the responsibility to settle the estate. It is very helpful if this person has a basic understanding of where all the assets are located so he or she can efficiently administer the estate. This person will need to gather all the assets, have them appraised, gather life insurance proceeds that were payable to the estate, pay debts and undertake many other similar duties. As executor, he or she will need to file a petition with the court to probate the estate and will also need to file income tax returns and estate tax returns. This position of executor ordinarily lasts for a few months before the court signs off on the will at the final hearing.

Having a valid will also allows for the designation of a guardian for any minor children. This is commonly one of the most difficult decisions that parents make when creating a will. But if a guardian is not chosen and both parents die, then the courts will pick a guardian. If it is hard for the parents to pick an appropriate person, just think how difficult it would be for the courts to pick someone whom the parents would have approved. Once a guardian is chosen, a discussion between the parents and the guardian should take place where the values with which the parents would want the children raised are discussed.

TRUSTEE

Only a will can designate a guardian for children. But a will does nothing to protect the assets of those children. A trust can be used to designate a person to watch over the children's assets. A trustee must be chosen to manage the assets that will be used for the benefit of the children. The trustee may or may not be the same person as the guardian. If an individual trustee is chosen, he or she will be involved in the children's lives for many years. This is not a short-term arrangement in most cases. It is not uncommon for the final distribution from a trust to be delayed until the children are age 40. This means that, depending on the age of the youngest child, the duties of the trustee may not end for nearly 40 years. This is also a position only for someone with the utmost integrity and a keen sense of responsibility.

Additionally, this person will need to safeguard, invest, administer and file tax returns according to the terms of the trust (which can be nothing more than the entity created by the will that spells out how and under what terms the money can be distributed to the children). This person must not only have the qualifications to be a trustee, but also the time.

In some cases, it is advisable to designate a corporate trustee (such as a bank). Corporate trustees follow very strict guidelines, and it is extremely rare for fiduciary responsibility to be breached. Corporate trustees are usually better-equipped to make decisions on an objective basis, rather than an emotional one. They generally have the expertise needed to avoid mistakes and the financial backing to correct mistakes if they are made. Trusts are also ongoing concerns, meaning that there will be someone to step in if the original trust officer dies. Continuity of management is assured.

CREDIT SHELTER TRUST

A credit shelter trust, also known as a bypass trust, is an instrument used to reduce the amount of estate taxes that is due at the death of the second spouse. It is commonly created inside a will and is funded only at the death of the first spouse. According to a current law, an unlimited amount of money can be transferred to a spouse without triggering any taxes, but this only delays the possible taxes until the death of the second spouse. In 2005, $1.5 million can be placed into a credit shelter trust; thus it is not subject to estate taxation at the death of the second spouse. It is designed specifically to allow the surviving spouse access to the funds, without those funds being included in that spouse's taxable estate at his or her death. It is normally advisable to have this type of trust in the estate plan of any couple with a combined net worth of $3 million, although it frequently makes sense to consider one even if the estate is worth less. (When calculating the value of the total estate, remember to include any life insurance not owned by a separate trust.)

POWER OF ATTORNEY

Wills are designed to give authority to an executor to deal with another person's affairs at death. But what happens if that person is just incapacitated?

A durable power of attorney grants someone (agent) the authority to act on your (principal's) behalf during your lifetime. It remains in effect both before and after an incapacitation. A power of attorney that is not durable will cease to be effective once the principal is incapacitated. (Some people prefer a springing power of attorney, which does not come into play until the principal is declared incompetent.)

It is usually advisable to have a durable power of attorney so that someone can act on your behalf in the event of a disability or incapacitation. Just because your investments are jointly owned does not give the non-disabled owner the right to sell the property. A durable power of attorney gives the agent the ability to make financial decisions and sign any documents relating to financial matters. The agent has the authority to conduct most financial business, with the exception of making gifts. Having this document in place allows you to determine the person who will follow your wishes the best. If it does not exist at the time of the disability, the courts will decide who should act on your behalf. It is more costly to have the courts deal with this issue, and the resulting delay could also prove to be expensive. All powers of attorney become ineffective at the death of the principal.

HEALTH-CARE POWER OF ATTORNEY

A health-care power of attorney grants the person designated as the agent the power to make most health-care decisions in the event the principal is not able to make the decisions. It takes effect only once the principal is determined to no longer have the capacity to make medical decisions.

LIVING WILLS

Living wills, also known as advance directives, authorize doctors to discontinue treatment if certain conditions are met. Living wills spell out under what circumstances the principal would not want his or her doctor to take action to prolong his or her life. For instance, if you have suffered a debilitating stroke and it is the opinion of your doctor that you will never recover and will remain on ventilators or some other medical device for the rest of your life, would you want the doctors to continue treatment?

LIVING TRUSTS

A living trust is a trust that is created during the lifetime of the grantor (the person who created the trust). It is a revocable trust, meaning that any assets that are placed inside the trust can be removed at any time, and the trust arrangement can be terminated any time the grantor chooses.

One of the major advantages of a living trust is its ability to avoid the probate process. Removing assets from the probate process will reduce estate-settlement expenses. At the death of the grantor, the trust becomes irrevocable and its contents pass by operation of law to the trust's beneficiary. The fact that the trust is not involved in the probate process also helps to transfer the assets to the beneficiary without public scrutiny. Wills become a matter of public record during the probate process. A living trust is a private document and therefore is not subject to public scrutiny.

Living trusts can play a very important role in estate planning. However, they do not provide any estate-tax reduction, nor do they provide any asset protection. These two limitations are commonly misunderstood. Since a living trust is revocable, its contents are deemed a part of the grantor's taxable estate. As such, the trust is not excluded from federal estate taxation. Also, since the grantor retains full control over the assets inside of the trust, the trust is not exempt from the grantor's creditors in the event of a bankruptcy.

FAMILY LIMITED PARTNERSHIPS

A family limited partnership (FLP) is, as the name implies, a limited partnership. A typical use of an FLP works like this: mom and dad create the FLP and transfer assets (such as a family business, real estate or investments) into it. Mom and dad structure the ownership such that they own one percent as general partners and 99 percent as limited partners. The general partner has unlimited liability but maintains control over the entire FLP. The limited partners retain liability only to the extent of their investment in the partnership but have no voice in the operation of the partnership. Generally, the one-percent ownership of the general partner will be held by another legal entity such as a limited liability corporation (LLC). This allows mom and dad to avoid any personal liability outside of the assets transferred to the FLP.

One of the reasons many parents resist giving away ownership in the family business is the loss of control. With an FLP, mom and dad can give away limited partnership shares while maintaining complete control via their ownership of the general partnership. This means that over time, mom and dad can give away the ownership of the business but still run it without interference.

Another advantage of an FLP is its ability to reduce estate taxes. Assets are valued at the fair market value, which is determined by what a willing buyer would pay a willing seller. Since FLPs are structured to limit the transfer of shares, a willing buyer would not be willing to pay full price for an asset that was not readily marketable. A common limitation in an FLP is to limit the ability of a limited partner to sell or transfer his or her shares except to a family member or with the consent of all other family members. Given this transfer limitation and the clear marketability limitation of a partnership, it is common to achieve a valuation discount of up to 20 percent to 40 percent. This ultimately means that when estate taxes are involved, the IRS will view the asset as worth 20 percent to 40 percent less than what it would have been without the FLP, and enormous estate-tax savings are achieved.

A final advantage of an FLP is in the area of asset protection. Generally, creditors of a partnership are not allowed to seize the assets of the partnership to satisfy a debt or judgment. Rather, they are restricted to a "charging order" against the assets of the partnership. The creditor is entitled to any distributions that the FLP makes to the partners. However, if no distributions are made, then the creditor will get a K-1 (partnership distribution form) for any income the FLP received. The creditor will then have to pay income taxes, but will not receive any cash from the FLP to pay them. While the charging order is in effect, the creditor gets no voting rights or control of the FLP. This usually drives the creditor to the bargaining table to settle for something far less than what the charging order required.

There are several disadvantages of an FLP: One is the start-up costs. It can cost $5,000 or more to establish the partnership. Another is the ongoing maintenance. It is necessary to file a separate FLP tax return each year. The

FLP must be run as a separate business and not just a checkbook for mom and dad. Personal and business finances must be kept completely separate. Finally, FLPs invite an IRS audit when the valuation discounts are taken at the death of a partner. Detailed procedures must be followed, and the advice and counsel of a CPA and attorney are essential.

ESTATE TAXES AND SOCIAL CAPITAL

Those who have accumulated assets that are sufficient to trigger estate taxes, even after the basic estate planning measures have been taken, must decide whether it is important for them to dictate how their "social capital" will be distributed after their deaths.

Whether you recognize it or not, your assets are viewed by the government in two distinct sections. One is the personal capital that belongs to you and then your heirs. The other is social capital that belongs to the government. The government does not call it "social capital," it calls it "estate taxes." We call it "social capital" because the money is going to be spent on social causes – either by you or by the government. Many people believe (and the government prefers it that way) that you have no say in how your social capital is spent. While it is true that the social capital will not be available to your heirs, it is not true that you no longer have control of it.

Ask yourself how important it is to determine for yourself how your social capital is used to improve society. Should the government use the money to fund social programs it deems worthy, or is it possible it would be better to give the money to a charitable organization that uses the money for causes that are near and dear to your heart? This question must be answered well in advance of death. If done properly, this type of planning can ensure that you are able to distribute your social capital during your lifetime and thereby enjoy witnessing the fruits of your labors. It all comes down to who you believe will do a better job of spending your money – you or the government.

There are a multitude of options when it comes to charitable planning. The best advice is to seek counsel with regard to your specific situation. Plan early and update often to achieve the most satisfying results.

CONCLUSION

In our financial planning practice, clients must have up-to-date estate plans that are reviewed by a qualified estate planning attorney every three years. We also recommend the use of several other techniques not addressed in this chapter due to their complexity.

As your estate continues to grow, an estate planning attorney will be a vital part of your planning team. Laws change all the time, which creates both problems and opportunities. Having a financial planning team looking out for you can be your most valuable asset.

CHAPTER 16

PROPERTY AND CASUALTY INSURANCE

One of the most neglected areas in financial planning is property and casualty insurance. Most experts agree that the first line of defense against a financial catastrophe involving your assets is properly planning your insurance coverage.

Case in Point

Wesley and Angela had recently sold their small, privately-held business and received $4 million after income taxes and all the other costs associated with the sale. Both were in their mid-60s and had planned that the proceeds from the sale of their business would provide for a comfortable retirement.

After receiving the $4 million, Wesley and Angela hired a money manager and invested in a conservative portfolio of stocks and bonds. They wanted to minimize investment risk due to their ages and the fact that they had sold their business, which had been their only income source. Without the business, Wesley and Angela had limited ability to ever accumulate significant assets again.

About a year after the sale, things were working out just as planned. Unfortunately, Angela was involved in an automobile accident with a pedestrian. Angela said that the person she hit stepped off of the curb right in front of her. The pedestrian said that Angela jumped the curb and hit him.

As expected, the accident ended up in a lawsuit. At the end of the trial, the jury awarded the pedestrian, who was now in a wheelchair, $3 million. Wesley and Angela owned a $1 million umbrella insurance policy which paid the policy limits to the pedestrian. The other $2 million would have to be paid out of the investment account.

Unfortunately, this left Wesley and Angela with only $1 million and forced Wesley to go back to work managing a small manufacturing company.

As you can see, a lifetime of work can disappear in a flash without proper planning. Wesley and Angela did not *actively* choose to assume the risk that they did. But by not planning properly, they *passively* chose to self-insure. They did not fully understand that this situation could have been completely avoided.

The following is a summary of different types of property and casualty insurance and what actions should be taken to properly plan for potentially large losses:

HOMEOWNER'S INSURANCE

There are several types of basic homeowner's policies. Each one is designed to cover different risks for different situations. Some policies are designed to cover named perils, and others are designed to cover all perils except those specifically excluded. Others are designed for renters, who do not need coverage for the structure itself, but need their property insured and also need liability coverage.

One priority for any homeowner is to make certain that adequate coverage on the structure itself is maintained. Most policies have a co-insurance clause that requires the homeowner to maintain coverage of at least 80 percent of the replacement cost of the home at the time of loss. This makes it essential to have an updated replacement cost analysis done to make certain proper coverage is maintained. If the cost of replacement after a loss exceeds the 80 percent minimum coverage level, the insurance company will not be required to pay policy limits.

It works like this: If you have a policy with a limit of $500,000, but after a loss the cost to replace the structure is $750,000, then the insurance company will only pay $333,333.33 (excluding deductibles).

Insurance Amount	$500,000
Replacement Cost	$750,000
Percentage of coverage to actual loss	66.67% ($500,000 / $750,000)
Insurance pays	$500,000 x 66.67% = $333,333.33

The minimum amount of coverage in this case should have been:

Replacement Cost	$750,000
Minimum coverage %	80%
Necessary coverage	$600,000 ($750,000 x 80%)

If a coverage of $600,000 was in place, the insurance company would pay the policy limit of $600,000 (not the actual replacement of $750,000 because the policy limit still applies). However, this is still far better than having a policy with a $500,000 limit that will only pay $333,333.33 due to insufficient coverage.

Before assuming that you need coverage for the entire value of your home, don't forget to take into account that you can subtract the value of the land itself before determining the amount of coverage. Once you have established this figure, you should adjust it annually for the appropriate inflation in your area.

Another priority is to understand whether you have replacement-cost coverage or actual-cash-value coverage. Most policies cover the contents of your home at 40 percent to 60 percent of the amount for which your home is insured. This means that if you have a $500,000 policy, then the contents of the home are covered up to $200,000 to $300,000. The real issue is if the insurance company will only be paying the cost to replace your clothes, refrigerator, sofa, etc., or if it is going to give you the actual value of these items. If you will only receive the cash value, then you will go to a lot of garage sales to replace your items, or you will pay the difference out of pocket. Most people either don't have the cash available to add to the insurance money or would prefer not to have to spend it in that manner. Replacement coverage costs more, but is usually worth it.

The next issue becomes proving what items were in the house at the time of loss. When filing the claim with the insurance company, you must prove that you owned a specific item and establish its value. One thing that will go a long way in helping with this is to get out your camcorder and create a record of everything you owned at a specific time. Don't forget the closets, attic, under the staircase, basement, backyard shed, garage and off-site storage facility. Obviously, the tape should be kept off site in a safe deposit box or something similar. It is best to have a detailed inventory that includes when you purchased the item, how much was paid, the make and model, and a description. However, most people just are not going to take the time to do this since the contents of their homes are changing all the time. At least a video could help you get started on the right foot.

After completing this video, you may discover that 40 percent to 60 percent just won't cover all your possessions. In that case, you can purchase additional coverage. You should also take inventory of higher-priced items such as jewelry, artwork, furs, electronic equipment, computers, etc. Most policies do not provide extensive coverage for these items. An *endorsement* or *rider* to your policy will cover these items.

Yet another priority is to understand what homeowner's policies do not cover. Losses resulting from flood or earthquake are not covered. You may purchase these coverages for an additional cost. War and nuclear accidents are not covered. In the past, most policies would cover losses due to terrorism, but since the terrorist attacks of September 11, 2001, many policies are starting to specifically exclude this risk. There isn't much you can do to reduce your exposure to war, nuclear accidents or terrorism, but you should be aware of how they are treated under your insurance policies.

UMBRELLA INSURANCE

Umbrella insurance, also known as "excess liability insurance," is designed to provide coverage for liabilities that exceed the coverage provided under your homeowner's or auto insurance policy. It is only activated once the policy limit of your underlying coverage is surpassed. Most of the time, the insurance company providing the umbrella coverage will require that a minimum amount of coverage be maintained by the underlying policy – usually at least $300,000. Coverage is most often provided by the same insurance company as your home or auto insurance.

Of all the insurance coverages that we review for our clients, umbrella coverage is the one that is most often missing or seriously underrepresented. Most financial planners believe it is the responsibility of property and casualty insurance agents to discuss this issue with their clients and make certain that proper coverage is maintained. The fact is that it is almost never dealt with properly.

Another problem we see from time to time is that the proper amount of coverage was secured, but since that time the client has purchased a lake house or mountain home and failed to inform the insurance company providing the umbrella coverage. This can result in coverage being denied on a claim resulting at the new home. Also, we find that clients will create other entities, such as FLPs (family limited partnerships), that will own certain assets rather than the client owning them personally. This can also cause a claim to be denied because the umbrella policy may need to list those assets in order for coverage to be guaranteed.

The question of how much coverage you should maintain is not an exact science. We believe that everyone should own at least $1 million of coverage. We also believe that coverage should *at least* match a client's net worth up to $10 million. After that, it is discussed on a case-by-case basis.

The cost of the coverage is surprisingly low. The first $1 million of coverage will generally cost somewhere around $300 per year. This price will vary greatly depending on the specific risk factors that you have. If you have a couple of accidents or traffic tickets on your record, teenage drivers, bad credit history, etc., you will likely pay a lot more for your coverage. If you have teenage drivers with bad driving records, you may not be able to get coverage at all. The assistance of a qualified agent is invaluable to making sure adequate coverage is maintained.

AUTOMOBILE INSURANCE

The most important part of an automobile insurance policy is the liability coverage. It is so fundamental that most states require at least a minimal amount of coverage. The first step in understanding the liability coverage provided by an automobile insurance policy is to understand the terminology. The way the liability coverage is usually quoted is something like 20/40/10. This means that the policy covers $20,000 for bodily injury per person with a $40,000 maximum per accident and $10,000 worth of coverage for property damage per accident. These are the types of limits you normally see as the minimum required by a state.

These limits are not nearly sufficient for most people and certainly will not be high enough to meet the underlying liability coverage requirements of an umbrella policy. If you are involved in an accident that is determined to be your fault, and the resulting damage is for an amount that is higher than that covered by your policy, you are responsible for the difference. Therefore, it is normally advisable to have your policy limits raised to the maximum. You will likely be surprised that the cost is not that much more than the cost of minimum coverage.

Collision and comprehensive coverages are designed to take care of damage to your car. Collision coverage will pay to repair your car, up to policy limits, when you or someone driving your car caused the accident. Comprehensive coverage will pay to repair your car for damage that results from something other than an accident with another vehicle. Common examples are theft, vandalism, natural disasters, etc.

Both collision and comprehensive coverages come with a deductible – usually $250 to $1,000. Generally, it is advisable to have a deductible that is toward the higher end of the range. Over the past several years, the property and casualty insurance industry has become more and more challenging. What this has meant to the consumer is that many insurers are looking for reasons to drop coverage on people deemed a poor risk. Therefore, it has become far more likely than in the past that a couple of small fender-benders will cause the insurance company to drop you or, at the very least, raise your rates. Given this probability, we believe that higher deductibles are in order, since most people are more likely to pay for small claims of $1,000 or less out of their pocket and not involve the insurance company. And if you are going to pay for any small losses of $1,000 or less out of your pocket, then match your deductible to what you will actually do in the event of a loss. You will also reduce your premiums quite a bit by raising your deductible from $250 to $1,000.

Personal injury protection will pay medical expenses for you and anyone in your car injured during an accident. It pays regardless of who is at fault, but your insurance company will likely seek reimbursement from the other driver's insurance company if the other driver is determined to be at fault.

Uninsured/underinsured motorist coverage is designed to pay the medical bills and property damage that is caused by a driver who does not have insurance or does not have enough coverage to pay for the losses that have resulted from an accident. This coverage can also apply when the insured or a family member is injured as a pedestrian.

The importance of property and casualty insurance in an overall financial plan cannot be overemphasized. Make certain that your property and casualty agent is a proactive advisor who annually reviews your coverage. Things change, financial situations change – change is inevitable. Make sure your coverage changes with you.

CHAPTER 17

DOCUMENTS YOUR FINANCIAL PLANNER NEEDS AND WHY

Probably the worst part of creating any financial plan is gathering the necessary data. Most people hate doing this as much as going to the dentist to get a root canal. But, as the old saying goes – garbage in, garbage out.

Case in Point

One recent client, Barbara, resisted when asked to prepare a budget. We had asked repeatedly for several weeks if she had taken the time to create a list of her monthly expenses, only to be given the usual, "I'm too busy." She finally gave us an approximation of what she thought was her monthly budget, and we started working on her financial plan.

At the following planning meeting, we showed her the enormous impact inaccurate assumptions about her expenses could make on her plan. She finally began to really understand why we needed an accurate budget. She went home after the meeting and added up her monthly expenses for the last year from her credit card statements, checkbook register, etc. She was stunned to find out that her actual expenses were about 50 percent higher than she had originally thought. At our next financial planning meeting, we informed her that at her present rate of spending, she would be bankrupt early into her retirement. She was then compelled to make the necessary changes in her life to reduce her expenses to a level that the financial plan indicated would be acceptable.

Another client, Paul, did not believe that it was necessary for us to review his estate planning documents since he had hired a very expensive attorney from a downtown firm. At our urging, he gave us copies of his and his wife's wills and trusts. Upon reviewing the documents, we discovered that, in fact, the documents had never been signed (executed). We also discovered that the attorney had made a rather large *error and had created signature pages for the husband to sign the wife's will and the wife to sign the husband's will. In other words, proper execution of these documents was not possible because the signature pages were incorrect.*

A complete and comprehensive financial plan includes a variety of documents. The paragraphs that follow identify many of the documents that are needed. These documents are essential for a properly drafted financial plan.

PERSONAL FINANCIAL STATEMENT

If you don't have one, don't panic. Most people don't. If you do, you are a step ahead. Your financial planner should review this document so that he or she can get a good feel for exactly where you are, financially, right now. This document will reveal exactly how you have allocated your assets. Do you own a lot of real estate, company stock, or lots of cash? This is the starting point of a plan.

Table 17-1 is a simple example of how to create your own personal balance sheet. To measure successful wealth management, there must be a definitive starting point.

Each year when an annual review is performed, you will be able to track the growth of your net worth. One note of caution: automobiles and other depreciating assets typically should not be included as assets, except to the extent that they could be sold to eliminate the debt attached to them.

Table 17-1

PERSONAL BALANCE SHEET		
ASSETS		
Liquid Assets		
Checking Account	_____	
Savings Account	_____	
Bank Money Market Deposits	_____	
Bank Certificates of Deposit	_____	
Subtotal		_____
Investment Assets		
Brokerage Account (His)	_____	
Brokerage Account (Hers)	_____	
Brokerage Account (Joint)	_____	
Life Insurance Cash Value	_____	
Subtotal		_____
Retirement Assets		
401(k)	_____	
IRA	_____	
Deferred Compensation	_____	
Subtotal		_____
Lifestyle Assets		
Primary House	_____	
Vacation House	_____	
Subtotal		_____
TOTAL ASSETS		_____
LIABILITIES		
Mortgage Notes	_____	
Line of Credit	_____	
Miscellaneous Notes	_____	
TOTAL LIABILITIES		_____
NET WORTH		
Total Assets	_____	
Total Liabilities	_____	
TOTAL NET WORTH		_____

LIFESTYLE EXPENSES

These are otherwise known as a "budget." We avoid the "b" word because the connotation is that we are somehow going to put the client on an allowance and they will never have fun again. By saying "lifestyle expenses," clients understand that all we are trying to do is capture and clarify how much money they will need to become financially independent. This inevitably means that some people will need to reduce spending, while others will be able to confirm that their expenses are in line with their resources. Each plan is different, but if you don't know how much you want to spend, how do you know if you have enough? Table 17-2 is a simple form to help you gain an understanding of your current expenses.

Once you have completed this form, you will know how much money you need each month to make ends meet. You might also use this information to find ways to reduce expenses. Either way, now that you know what your needs are, you can work to accumulate enough assets to take care of them.

INVESTMENT ACCOUNT STATEMENTS

Everyone should get an unbiased view of his or her investment portfolio in its entirety. Each individual investment account will reveal exactly what and how much is owned. How many shares of XYZ stock or ABC fund do you own? How does this investment fit in your overall allocation? Are you heavily invested in any one area? Would it be possible to consolidate some accounts to reduce paperwork headaches and maybe reduce administration fees? These questions should be answered by a complete review of your investments. Once you understand exactly where you are, you can make changes, if needed, to create the right balance based upon your risk tolerance and time horizon.

RETIREMENT PLAN STATEMENTS

These should be a part of the above analysis, but there are additional items to review in these investments. What is the cost to administer the plan? Is it too high? What is your current tax bracket? Does it make sense to defer taxes if your tax bracket will be low this year or next or possibly higher in retirement? Does your employer match your investments? If not, is the fund selection adequate to create a good portfolio? How is the match calculated? These questions need to be answered so that you can be certain you are making the right choices.

Table
17-2

FAMILY LIFESTYLE EXPENSES		
Household Expenses	**Monthly**	**Annually**
Mortgage		
Groceries		
Home Repairs		
Landscaping		
Swimming Pool Upkeep		
Newspapers/Periodicals		
House Cleaning		
Home Security System		
Furnishings Allowance		
Subtotal		
Personal Expenses	**Monthly**	**Annually**
Dining Out		
Entertainment		
Dry Cleaning		
Clothing		
Personal Care		
Automobile Payment		
Auto Fuel & Upkeep		
Gifts		
Charitable Contributions		
Cellular Phone		
Medical & Dental Expenses		
Children's Allowances		
Vacation		
Miscellaneous		
Subtotal		
Utilities	**Monthly**	**Annually**
Electricity		
Gas		
Water/Sewer		
Home Telephone		
Cable TV		
Internet		
Subtotal		
Insurance	**Monthly**	**Annually**
Homeowner's Insurance		
Auto Insurance		
Umbrella Liability Insurance		
Health Insurance		
Life Insurance		
Disability Insurance		
Other Insurance		
Subtotal		
Taxes	**Monthly**	**Annually**
Payroll Taxes		
Federal Income Taxes		
State Income Taxes		
Real Estate & Property Taxes		
Subtotal		
Grand Total		

EMPLOYEE BENEFITS BOOKLET

Do you understand the benefits that your employer is providing? Most people say "no," and those who say "yes" don't usually understand them as well as they think they do.

a) **Group Disability** – This type of insurance pays an employee a monthly income if the employee becomes sick or hurt and is unable to work, normally after about 90 days. A typical policy will pay until the disabled worker turns 65, as long as the definition of disabled is met, which is normally very restrictive. Do you understand exactly how much you would receive if you were disabled? Does your plan cover 60 percent of wages? How are wages defined? Does it include commissions or bonuses? Is the benefit taxable? Are you aware that while most plans cover around 60 percent, the maximum is capped at $5,000 to $10,000 per month? At a $5,000 monthly cap, anyone making more than $100,000 is not covered for 60 percent. If commissions or bonuses are not covered, then the situation is much worse than you might have thought. Also, this type of coverage normally does not include coverage for pension or profit-sharing accounts. This means that if you become disabled and can find a way to reduce your lifestyle expenses down to whatever the coverage amount is, what will you do when you turn 65 and have not been able to fund your retirement plan or become vested in the company pension?

b) **Group Life Insurance** – Are you paying for life insurance offered through the company? Are you aware of how high the rates usually are due to adverse selection? Adverse selection is created when anyone can purchase insurance without evidence of insurability. Those whose health is the poorest will opt to take out the most insurance they can, while those who are healthy will go out and price their own policies to see if they can get coverage cheaper. Those who can will buy individual coverage, which leaves only those in the poorest health in the group insurance pool, thus creating the adverse selection. Most of the time, if you are healthy, it makes more sense to purchase your own policy outside of the company. Furthermore, are you aware that most of the time you can't take the group policy with you when you leave the company? This can create a very bad situation if you become uninsurable and then need to leave the company. You do not want to be stuck in a job you don't like just because you will lose your life insurance if you leave.

c) **Group Health Insurance** – If your company offers several choices, be sure to take the time to analyze each option to determine which one would work best for you. If you and your family are healthy, then you should consider the higher deductible, higher co-pay plan. If you have chronic health problems, then select the plan with the low deductible and low co-pay. How much are you paying for the company's group health insurance plan to cover you and your family? If you and/or your family are healthy, it might make financial sense to consider paying for your own individual health plan outside of the company. The premiums would most likely not be deductible, but group health insurance is becoming so outrageously priced due to adverse selection that the lack of a tax deduction might not matter.

d) **Flexible Spending Accounts** – Are you taking advantage of a flexible spending account (FSA)? FSAs allow you to reduce your taxable income by placing money in the FSA that you will use to pay for healthcare and dependent-care expenses. You do have to jump through a few hoops to achieve the tax reduction, but if you are planning a medical procedure that is not covered by your health plan (i.e. laser eye surgery), the savings can be substantial. If you are paying for childcare, this decision is a no-brainer.

LIFE INSURANCE POLICIES

All life insurance policies need to be reviewed periodically. As mortality rates have continued to drop, life insurance rates have dropped as well. Many times, annually renewable term (ART) policies, which increase in premiums each year, can be replaced with 10-, 15- or 20-year level-term policies for around the same price currently being paid for ARTs. Over the 10-, 15- or 20-year life of the policy, substantial savings can be achieved.

What is the current projection for your permanent life insurance? An "in-force ledger" should be run periodically to determine if the current premium being paid is adequate to keep the policy in force for your life expectancy. An in-force ledger will illustrate how your policy will perform given current assumptions as to mortality, interest rates, dividends, etc. It is not a guarantee of how the policy will perform. It is just the insurance company's best estimate as of right now. It could be substantially different than when you took the policy out originally. It could be that there is plenty of cash value, and you could reduce or even stop paying premiums now or in the near future. Conversely, you might find out that, given current assumptions, your policy will lapse soon. Finding out sooner rather than later is always better.

Does your policy have a disability waiver so that you do not have to pay premiums in the event of a disability? Does your beneficiary designation in your insurance policy coordinate with that in your estate plan? Do you have your minor children listed as beneficiaries or contingent beneficiaries for your plan? If so, you shouldn't. Minors can't take legal ownership of life insurance proceeds; therefore, the insurance company will only release the funds to a court-appointed guardian. This will cause an unnecessary delay and create an added expense.

Life insurance can be complicated and should be dealt with proactively.

INDIVIDUAL DISABILITY POLICIES

As compared to group disability policies, individual disability policies are far less restrictive and provide much better coverage. Even so, individual disability policies being issued today are usually not nearly as comprehensive as policies issued several years ago. If you have an older policy, make certain that you pay the premiums timely. You do not want to allow an older policy to lapse.

Check your policy carefully. How does the policy define disability? Is mental health covered? Do you have inflation protection? Have you reviewed the coverage you have and the amount you *currently* need? Do you know how much you need? Can your policy be canceled? Is your policy guaranteed renewable?

LONG-TERM CARE POLICY

Most people don't have long-term care policies but should. If you do own one, there are several things you should make certain are part of the policy. One of the defining elements of a long-term care policy is the inflation protection. If your policy benefit does not inflate each year, then by the time you actually qualify for benefits the coverage amount will be inadequate (and probably by a large margin).

Does your policy allow you to receive care in your home? Does the policy include a daily, weekly or monthly benefit? Each of these benefits can have a different outcome, and you should understand each. Is your policy a lifetime-pay or a limited-pay (such as 10 years) policy? Does the insurance company have a history of raising rates? Is the company highly rated by more than one rating service?

There is little about long-term care that is simple, and the benefits can be confusing. Take the time to understand what you have and what you need.

HOME MORTGAGE

Your home may be one of your biggest assets. Be sure you understand the ins and outs of your mortgage. Is the rate on your mortgage competitive? Would it make sense to refinance? How much longer do you plan to live in your house? Are you paying for private mortgage insurance (PMI) even though you now have at least 20 percent equity in your home? If you add money to each monthly payment, how much sooner could you retire your mortgage?

INCOME-TAX RETURNS

An amazing amount of information can be gleaned from an income-tax return. For instance, you may not remember to tell your planner about a carry-forward loss on the stock you sold a couple of years ago. Did you file a form 709 for the money you contributed to an irrevocable trust? Does your CPA even know that you have a trust? Would it make sense to reduce your interest income in favor of tax-free income? Did you itemize your deductions and include a deduction for the clothing you gave to charity?

ESTATE PLANNING DOCUMENTS

Your wills, trusts and ancillary documents (such as power of attorney and advanced directives) should be reviewed by a qualified estate planning attorney at least every five years. A review should be done sooner if any significant changes take place (such as a death, divorce, marriage, adoption, etc.).

One of the most significant questions you need to ask is whether there is coordination between your estate planning and your investment account titling and beneficiary designations. More often than you would think, there is a problem in probating an estate as the deceased had wished because there was no coordination between the estate plan and the titling of assets and beneficiary designations.

For example, you may have created a will that gives specific bequests to family members, friends or even a trust, but if all your assets have beneficiary designations, then there won't be any money to fund those bequests. Also, if you have your investment accounts titled as "joint with rights of survivorship," then when one of the account holders dies, all the assets become the property of the survivor. This means that the deceased person can't determine where his or her half of the account will go because it is already gone.

Have you thought about the person you designated as your children's guardian or trustee in the event of your death and whether that person is still the best choice? If you have established a trust, have you funded it? If you made gifts to the trust, did you file the proper paperwork with your tax returns?

HOMEOWNER'S INSURANCE

This type of coverage not only protects your home, but normally protects your household furnishings as well. It usually has a certain amount of personal liability coverage to protect you in the event that someone is injured on your property.

Does your policy cover replacement costs? If you own a home in a high-growth area, you need to make certain that your total coverage amount is in line with the value of your home. Most people are not aware that a homeowner must insure his or her home for at least 80 percent of the replacement cost. If a home is insured for less than 80 percent, then the insurance company will not have to pay the full coverage amount.

For example, if you have a home that would cost $200,000 to replace and you only have it insured for $150,000, then you only have 75 percent coverage. This means that the insurance company would only pay $112,500 ($150,000 x 75%) in the event of a total loss.

What is the deductible for your homeowner's policy? Given the state of the property and casualty insurance industry, it is not advisable to involve the insurance company in small claims. And if you are not going to use your insurance for a small claim, then why would you pay the high cost of a low deductible?

AUTOMOBILE INSURANCE

Most states require that a minimum amount of insurance be carried on automobiles. If you are carrying the minimums, then you are most likely very underinsured. State minimums are just that – minimums. Most people should carry several times the minimum.

Minimums can be as low as $25,000 per accident. If you are at fault in an accident that involves an expensive luxury car or possibly involves additional property, such as a building, the total loss can be much higher than $25,000. The additional loss in excess of $25,000 will have to be paid from your personal assets. Don't worry about how much it will increase your premiums. The minimum amount of coverage is usually the most expensive. Doubling or tripling your coverage limits should not come close to doubling or tripling your premiums. Is your deductible $250 to $500? If so, raise it to $1,000. It is no longer advisable to make a claim for a small loss. Your rates will likely go up, or, even worse, you could get dropped altogether. Use the savings from raising the deductible to increase your coverage amounts.

UMBRELLA INSURANCE POLICY

Do you have one? You should. Umbrella insurance is your first line of defense to protect your assets should a large claim come your way. These policies, also known as "personal liability insurance," are designed to cover losses that exceed the total limits of your automobile and homeowner's policies. It is inexpensive coverage to have (usually around $300 per year for $1 million of coverage), and most everyone should have it. Since most homeowner's policies have a liability limit of $300,000, you need to have insurance that will cover you for liabilities that rise above that amount.

You also need to make certain that the policy you own covers the type of risk that you most likely could encounter. Does the policy cover just you, or does it cover other people as well? This distinction can make a huge difference if a friend is driving your boat and injures someone, for example. Are you covered? You need to know before a claim is made.

BUY/SELL AGREEMENT

If you own a business, do you have a buy/sell agreement? If you have one, is it funded? How is the value of the business determined if one of the triggering events takes place? Is it still a fair way to evaluate the value of your company? If it is not funded, how will the surviving owner(s) be able to pay the family of the deceased owner? Does the agreement address what happens if an owner is disabled? What about in cases of divorce? How is the retirement of owners planned for? These questions need to be answered long before anything goes wrong.

This is certainly not a complete list of all documents your financial planner might need. It is just a very good start. Each plan will require specific information unique to each particular individual. As you can see, there are lots of questions that need answers. And taking a proactive approach can save a lot of heartache down the road. Don't allow chance to play a role in your financial life – become proactive.

CHAPTER 18

CONCLUSION

Time is running out for you, like all of us. The countdown is ticking whether or not we choose to face it. People take action for one of two reasons: either they are uncomfortable and will do anything to give themselves relief, or the action makes so much sense there is no reason not to act. Prosprus falls into the latter category.

Over the years, we have completed planning for business owners, executives and professionals who, for whatever reasons, had procrastinated for years. We made sense of their financial matters, and our systems for both design and implementation motivated them to start, finish and continue to stay the course.

With the aging of baby boomers, increasing consumer demands and improved technology, the financial services and products available today are the finest ever offered. But as with everything else, these products, services and concepts are more sophisticated and more complex, and still require intelligent, capable, honest providers to communicate, implement and sometimes administer these solutions.

It is our firm belief that Prosprus can change the way planning is done in the future – in favor of the customer. We hope that many financial services professionals will read this book and that they will come to the same realization we have: the planning industry must apply the technology professionals already use to put planning back where it belongs, into the hands of the client.

We are simply guides to assist clients in determining their objectives, maintaining realism, implementing agreed-upon recommendations and providing a sounding board. Finally, we are someone to trust, someone who will watch their backs. A financial planner who understands his or her client will guide that client toward the solutions that will bring peace of mind. We can't stop the countdown, but we can help relieve our clients' fears.

Consolidation in financial services is still in the early stages of its development, and the players – banks, insurance companies, brokerage firms and accounting firms – are still trying to figure out where they fit. Frankly, it will take some time for things to settle out. Therefore, finding providers who are grounded in their specialties will still require some effort on your part. The good news is that the sophistication requirement allows no room for mediocrity, and the attrition rate for the poorly educated and unprofessional is accelerating – all to the benefit of the customer.

A man was walking along a path heading for a town several miles down the road. He came to a fork in the road. It was marked so that it appeared either of the roads could be taken to the same destination. Another man happened to be standing at the fork, leaning against a fence. Upon noticing the bystander, the first man looked at the second and asked, "Does it matter which one of these roads I take?" The bystander replied, "Not to me, it doesn't."

Well it does matter to us. The road you take is going to make a difference to you and your legacy. Your destination may be financial independence, or it may be financial ruin. It can provide opportunity money for future generations or goodwill for years to come because you are charitably inclined. It does matter what road you take, and we wish you well on your journey. Keep in mind – time is running out.

ABOUT THE AUTHORS

Randall N. Smith
Managing Principal
Smith, Frank & Partners, LLC

As managing principal at a major firm, Randall Smith has spearheaded development of a breakthrough system for financial planning. By leveraging technology previously hidden from clients' view, Smith helps his clients accurately visualize how today's financial decisions will impact their future.

Smith oversees operations of Smith, Frank & Partners, LLC, which offers businesses and individuals everything from financial planning and retirement planning to investments and insurance. To introduce busy executives to the financial planning process, Smith writes a column for the CEO IQ micronewspaper and speaks to groups across the nation.

Smith is a registered representative with NFP Securities, Inc. He graduated from Dallas Baptist University with a bachelor's degree. He holds several licenses and designations, including Chartered Life Underwriter, Series 6 registration for mutual funds and variable products, and Series 63 registration for the Uniform Securities Agent State Law Exam.

Gregory L. Reed
Director of Planning
Smith, Frank & Partners, LLC

After seeing the difficulty many clients had connecting their current actions to their financial futures, Greg Reed co-developed with Randy Smith a breakthrough system for financial planning.

Reed specializes in structuring financial plans for high-net-worth individuals and business owners. Experienced in both financial planning and information technology, he acts as both financial planner and educator. Reed works with complex planning techniques and brings them to life for the client.

Reed earned a bachelor's degree in business administration from The University of Texas at Arlington, as well as a master's degree in business administration from Dallas Baptist University. He is a registered representative with NFP Securities, Inc. Reed holds several licenses and designations, including Series 7 registration for general securities, Series 63 registration for the Uniform Securities Agent State Law Exam, Series 66 for Uniform Combined State Law Exam and Series 24 for General Securities Principal. He is a CERTIFIED FINANCIAL PLANNER™ practitioner, Chartered Life Underwriter and Certified Fund Specialist.

INDEX

E

Education IRA 75
Employee benefits booklet 96
  flexible spending accounts 97
  group disability 96
  group health insurance 96
  group life insurance 96
Endorsement 87
Equity 51
Estate planning 77
  corporate trustee 79
  credit-shelter trust 80
  estate taxes 83
  Family Limited Partnership (FLP)
    81
  health-care power of attorney 81
  living trusts 81
  living wills 81
  power of attorney 80
  social capital 83
  trustee 79
  will 78
Estate taxes 83
Excess liability insurance. *See*
    Umbrella insurance
Excuses 12
Execution 31
Executor 78

F

Family Limited Partnership (FLP) 81
Fee-only advice 8
Fees and commissions 8
Financial independence 41, 42, 74
Financial lifecycle 16, 17
Flexible spending accounts 97
Forrester, Inc. 7
Future value 49
Future-time dollars 9

G

Grantor 81
Graphs
  Graph 10-1 42

Graph 10-2 43
Graph 10-3 44
Graph 12-1 57
Graph 12-2 58
Graph 13-1 66
Graph 13-2 67
Graph 13-3 68
Graph 9-1 38
Graph 9-2 39
Group disability 96
Group health insurance 96
Group life insurance 96
Guardian 79

H

Health-care power of attorney 81
Home mortgage 98
Homeowner's insurance 86, 99
  endorsement 87

I

Ibbotson Associates 52
Income tax returns 99
Individual disability policies 98
Inflation 45
Insurance 85
  automobile 89, 100
  disability 96, 98
  health 96
  homeowner's 86, 99
  life 55, 97
  long-term care 63, 98
  property and casualty 85
  umbrella 88, 100
Interest 51
Investment account statements 94
Investments 53
  bond 50
  stocks 50

L

Large-cap stock 50
Laws of intestacy 78
Life insurance 55, 56, 57, 59

U

W